PASTORAL BEREAVEMENT COUNSELING

PASTORAL BEREAVEMENT COUNSELING
A Structured Program to Help Mourners

Rabbi Jacob Goldberg

HUMAN SCIENCES PRESS, INC.

Acknowledgment is made to National Academy Press for permission to quote from Osterweis, M., Solomon, F., & Green, M., *Bereavement: Reactions, Consequences, and Care*, 1984.

Human Sciences Press is a subsidiary of
Plenum Publishing Corporation
233 Spring Street
New York, N.Y. 10013

Printed in the United States of America

Library of Congress Cataloging in Publication Data

Goldberg, Jacob, 1923–
    Pastoral bereavement counseling : a structured program to help mourners / by Jacob Goldberg.

    p.   cm.
    Bibliography: p.
    Includes index.
    1. Church work with the bereaved.   I. Title.
BV4330.G65   1988
259′.6—dc 19   87-30131 CIP
ISBN 0-89885-419-9

Halleluya, it is good to sing to God, it is pleasant to sing praises to Him . . . He heals the broken-hearted, He binds up their wounds.

—Psalms 147, 1 and 3

CONTENTS

ACKNOWLEDGMENTS

Many persons and organizations have played an important role over the past 14 years in the development of Pastoral Bereavement Counseling. While we cannot enumerate all of them in this space, we wish to acknowledge a debt of gratitude to those whose contributions were centrally significant:

Rabbi Paul Hait, Executive Vice-President of The New York Board of Rabbis, a colleague and mentor for many years, whose advice, support, and encouragement carried us through many critical junctures; the late Rabbi Harold H. Gordon of blessed memory, past Executive Director of The New York Board of Rabbis, was the first to recognize the great need for the program; Dr. Austin H. Kutscher, President of The Foundation of Thanatology at Columbia Presbyterian Hospital never failed to provide needed guidance on both the clinical and community aspects of the program; Father Howard Dalton, past Director of the Family Consultation Service of the Catholic Archdiocese of New York, helped gain acceptance for the concept by the wider pastoral community; J. David Seay, General Secretary and Counsel of the United Hospital Fund of Greater New York, whose early interest in the project guided us to a Special

Project Grant; Rabbi Isaac Trainin, former Director of the Department of Religious Affairs of the Federation of Jewish Philanthropies, for his help in arranging a 2-year grant from the Federation; Andrew Fier and Martin Kasdan, who helped us garner the interest and support of the funeral industry; Jeffrey Richards, for his charitable contributions in memory of his beloved mother, Helen Richards; Evelyn Roberts, for her charitable contributions in memory of her beloved husband, Robert H. Roberts; Isabelle Sklar, Associate Director of the Department of Social Work of Beth Israel Medical Center; Phyllis Mervis, of the Department of Social Work of Mt. Sinai Medical Center, for their guidance in clinical supervision; Rabbi Charles Spirn, Head Chaplain of Mt. Sinai Medical Center, for his interest and encouragement; and Major Dorothea McGowan, Director of Pastoral Care at Booth Memorial Hospital, for her interest and encouragement.

My work has been deeply influenced by counseling experiences with many mourner-clients. I have learned from them and from clergy colleagues who were students in the training courses I have conducted. All have had a positive influence on the evolution of Pastoral Bereavement Counseling. I think of them but cannot name them.

I thank my dear wife Helen, for all her wisdom, love, and patience. Without her neither the program nor this book would have come into being.

Most of all, I thank the God who made my life and career possible. As it is written (Deuteronomy 8, 17, and 18), "You might say in your heart, it is *my* power and the strength of *my* hand that has achieved for me this success. But you would do well to remember the Lord your God, for it is *He* who gives you the strength to achieve and to succeed."

Jacob Goldberg

This volume is respectfully dedicated to the blessed memory of our dear parents,

Hyman Goldberg
Miriam Goldberg
Jacob L. Rosenwasser
Bessie Marx Rosenwasser

Chapter 1

LOOKING FOR A BETTER WAY

Did you ever want to help a grief-stricken person? And didn't know how? Have you ever felt your heart going out towards a mourner, wanting to alleviate his pain or her sorrow? And wondered how to go about it—or whether you might be hurting more by trying to help?

In addition to wondering how to help, you might be aware of inner conflicting feelings. You might feel some hesitation. After all, dealing with a mourner can be a palpably painful process. Your own fears and your own accommodations with the mystery of death will necessarily become involved. It's a risky business; you might stir up inner personal complications.

On the other hand, you could be very useful to a fellow mortal. You and your loved ones are mortal too. Someday you might need someone else to counsel you.

If you became an effective helper, you would make a real difference in someone's life. You might also be deepening your inner empathy and sharpening your personal sensitivity in a basic area of living.

"But I wouldn't know what to do," you might say. "Yes, I'd like to relieve someone's pain, but how?"

The purpose of this book is to answer this question, to show that there is a way—and also—to introduce the possibility of setting up networks of bereavement counselors in American communities. The purpose of this book is to explain how effective programs for mourners can be instituted in any community that recognizes the need.

Now that we've gone through the birth pangs of establishing a Pastoral Bereavement Counseling program in New York, we can see its adoption by other communities as equally feasible and beneficial. We have seen that our program provides significant aid to those mourners who need emotional support and are not receiving any.

We have also witnessed some of the spiritual and psychological rewards that are reaped by counselors who volunteer their empathy and therapeutic skills. They are granted a new sense of genuine usefulness, and gain a heightened recognition of God's essential goodness. They can see a miracle happening before their eyes.

This is the premium aspect of Pastoral Bereavement Counseling. It provides benefits to all who participate—the mourners, the volunteer counselors, the professional administrators and supervisors, and the community sponsors.

Our work in New York has pioneered a way to recruit empathic persons to become interested in this field, to encourage them to learn proven methods and effective techniques. We now know that it is possible to motivate them to contribute their time and emotional energy to supporting bereaved persons in their community. Many people are beginning to see this as an enterprise that is beneficial to people and pleasing to God.

We are suggesting that the establishment of Pastoral Bereavement Counseling in New York may be seen as a pilot project for instituting it in other communities. Our hope is that this book will interest enough people to help us spread it nationally. Our prayer is that this work will ultimately go a great distance towards healing the wounds of the bereaved.

At this point, we can imagine some readers' reactions to this statement of purpose.

"Who needs it? Sure, it's tough to go through the shock and pain of losing a loved one, but that's life. People have to learn to live with it, and just be strong about it. In the end, time will heal and life goes on."

Whoever feels this way will obviously not want to become a mourner's counselor. But wait, before you close the book and walk away from the problem; perhaps you might ask yourself, "Why am I responding in this way? Why did I even pick up a book with this title or open its pages?"

Clearly, there's something about the subject that interests you. You may not want to become a counselor, but you feel intrigued and want to learn. To be interested in death, to wonder how it feels to lose one close to you, is perfectly normal and legitimate—*because awareness of death is inextricably connected with awareness of life.* Thinking of death is morbid only when you can think of nothing else.

Indeed, some theorists of the human condition suggest that the seemingly natural reaction—to flee from thinking about death—is actually counterproductive. They see the conscious denial of reality as a thwarting of the natural process of coping. Their thesis is that the opposite is right, that open acknowledgment of the ultimate reality of death is the *only path* to health and spiritual wholeness.

Ernest Becker (1973), in his *The Denial of Death,* asks us to consider whether a good part of man's spiritual and psychological ills might not derive from our futile efforts to escape from the terror of death. He suggests that we would do better if we conditioned ourselves to be aware of our fears.

We might be healthier if we began to acknowledge the certainty of not living forever. We might heighten our sense of the preciousness of love precisely to the degree that we accept an ever-present possibility of losing that love.

If you've opened this book and are reading these words, I'd like to encourage you to read further. I think it will benefit you and your loved ones. It can be healthy and liberating and life-enhancing.

What might be some reasons for people taking the attitude, "It's tough, but time will heal, it's no concern of mine"? I can think of two.

The first is that they may be responding this way because of vague fears about their own unclear feelings. They might be deciding that it's safer to keep the lid on. They may be frightened that by opening themselves to someone else's deep feelings they will be increasing their vulnerability to the hidden terror within themselves.

Falling back on the conventional "It's tough, but there's nothing can be done about it" attitude may simply be a way to avoid experiencing powerful emotions. It may be a socially accepted cop-out since we see so many people using it. But it's a lame excuse that can result in diminishing our emotional capacities.

The second reason is that people may be blindly accepting the prevailing notion that there is no remedy for mourners. The average person thinks that the only way is the stoic way. The respected wisdom is that the only way to go through bereavement is to "take it on the chin."

Our purpose in seeking to spread our movement is to overturn this notion. We believe that help and healing are *possible*; and that most communities can make them *available* for many mourners.

Pastoral Bereavement Counseling does not offer a cure in the sense of promising a complete cessation of pain. On the other hand, it is much more than a Band-Aid. It is a therapeutic process that can shorten the journey through traumatic stress. For many mourners it has been a Godsend.

Our program is based on the conviction that neither death nor the painful feelings engendered in the survivor are to be regarded as a taboo subject. We do not hide from the stress and the trauma of grief; but we are convinced that *there is a healthy way to manage and to treat it.* We believe our program can be a blessing for both the counselor and the mourner.

In this book we will describe how our movement was initiated and how it evolved. We will offer a model of operation, and invite emulation of our New York program by other communities.

We will explain the theoretical dynamics that underlie our particular approach, and present the clinical experiences over the past 10 years that demonstrate its effectiveness. We see our program as a pioneering effort, and would like to explicate its unique features.

HOW THE PROGRAM EVOLVED

I suppose it all began more than a half century ago, when I was a young lad of seven. My father died in 1930 at the age of forty-eight—suddenly, and in the space of a few hours. The memory of my mother's wails that night, pleading with God not to make her a young widow, and my sudden designation as a "tender orphan" by the concerned and commiserating neighbors, was forever seared into my conscious and unconscious mechanisms of adaptation.

I could not have known then, nor was there any conscious recognition during the subsequent 55 years of my life, that those events played a central dynamic role in my personal and professional development. It is only in the past year or so that I have begun to be aware of the pervasive influence those few hours probably had on the rest of my life.

I now see that it is quite possible that much of the personal manner in which I have as a rabbi conducted more han 3,000 funerals and preached hundreds of sermons on remembering the dead, derives from that childhood experience.

I now perceive that the special intensity that I brought to this area of living, and my heart-and-soul involvement in developing the program of structured bereavement counseling, may very well have been part of a lifelong "working through" of my early loss.

What were my feelings when my middle brother whispered in my ear that early Sunday August morning, "Jackie, wake up, our poppa has died"? I've never forgotten the distinct Yiddish words he used.

What were my feelings when I was brought into the room to approach my father's dead body to say good-bye and to ask forgiveness? (His face was covered, but I could see his physical presence. . . . What is dead, anyway?) I remember that my mother was tearing her hair and being restrained by neighbors, that my brother and sisters were sobbing. What was I supposed to do? How did they expect me to act?

I understand now, many years later, that my father's death, which I comprehended at that time in a very fragmentary way, deeply affected my entire being. It initiated a chain of psychological development that produced the intense empathy I have drawn from in my rabbinic ministrations for these 40 years. It may have been my private fountainhead from which poured forth a near-enthusiastic willingness to become emotionally involved with others' sorrows.

As I look back upon it, I do not remember being consciously sad. I remember my childhood years as being interesting and active. I was a top student and valedictorian at graduation from elementary school. I excelled in high school, winning scholarships and awards, and was elected president of the Student Organization. I recall a number of intimate friends and many acquaintances. I felt loved and cared for by my mother and siblings and extended family.

Yet, underneath it all, there was the constant reservoir of sadness. I experienced a status of differentness imposed by the unspoken label of "orphan," a vague difficulty in self-identification and an attenuation of self-worth. Because I was the "Jackie without a father" I was not completely one of the crowd. Even worse, it was not my doing and there was no way I could climb out of it.

I remember that I found some refuge in fantasizing. My late adolescence was characterized by an inordinate amount of daydreaming. Was that the childhood equivalent of the denial that operates in the adult bereavement process? I suppose so, but I didn't know it at the time.

During my junior year in college, my addiction to daydreaming and procrastination affected my studies drastically. I was probably unconsciously utilizing the same mechanism for fleeing from frustration in my scholastic endeavors that I had unconsciously employed in softening the pain of my father's absence. But there was no way I could have seen the connection at that time.

My father had been a pious and God-fearing man. My grandfather, who lived 4 years beyond his son's death, was a congregational and scholarly rabbi, with a stern philosophic insistence that religious Jews may not question God's decrees. Yet, my mother could not entirely hide her anger, and obliquely challenged God's wisdom.

She would often say to me when no one else was listening,

(perhaps as a minor I was a suitable sounding board in whose presence she could safely ventilate), "At least, why didn't God give me a warning about Poppa? Why did He take him so quickly, so suddenly, with one blow? He didn't let me prepare myself for this *umglick,* this misfortune."

My bar mitzvah celebration, 6 years after my father's death, was a Sabbath of tension between "Mazel tov" and "Where is Poppa? Why didn't he live to see this?" I remember that weekend as a microcosm of my family's conflicting reactions in the bereavement process we were all going through. We were all caught in the tension of opposing emotions.

On the one hand, we needed to express the sensible joy of family success and progress, the love of life and thanks to God. On the other hand, our spirits were suffused with anger and guilt, with the unexpressed and inexpressible frustration at the tragic turn of events.

Outwardly my childhood years appeared normal; inwardly they were subtly incomplete and distorted. Perhaps the success I achieved in later life was fueled by the need for completion of status that I had missed as a child. Perhaps this, as well as the definite hunger for peer approval that may have tilted my career choice towards the rabbinate, was derived from my unconscious yearning for healing and wholeness.

My mother's sickness and slow death was the second experience in bereavement for me, different than the first. My mother suffered from amyotropic lateral sclerosis (Lou Gehrig's Disease), a progressively debilitating illness that destroys the ability of the body's nervous system to regulate our vital processes. For 5 agonizing years her physical condition inexorably regressed as she lost the functions of her vital organs, beginning with her legs and finally reaching to her lungs and heart.

Her suffering and death, one month before I was ordained as the third of her sons to become a rabbi, became a lifelong personal challenge to become religiously reconciled to God's seeming injustices.

Throughout all my subsequent years I have never received an emotionally satisfying answer to meet this challenge. I have heard many philosophic explanations, even some that are very interesting and logical, but none that made it possible for me to maintain a completely comfortable and trusting relationship with God.

Mother herself had a brilliant philosophic answer. As she was beginning to face the horror and hopelessness of her illness, she confided to me, "You see, Jackie, this is God's answer to me. I complained that God took Poppa away suddenly and without warning—so now He's showing me the other way, long and painful. He's giving me the warning that he didn't give Poppa, and He's answering my lifelong complaint."

This seems to be an eminently logical explanation of a tragic coincidence in my parents' lives and deaths. While it can and does appeal to my mind, it doesn't jibe with my need to believe in God's goodness.

The fact that I've remembered this exchange about God's justice for all these years and still continue to smart under its essential irony, indicates my lifelong need to find peace in confronting bereavement. Perhaps it is because I've needed it for myself for so long that I have a parallel need to help others reach it.

By the time I started to officiate at congregants' funerals as a rabbi, my emotional orientation in this area had evolved quite a distance. My professional activities were unavoidably influenced by the legacy of both my parents' deaths. Instinctively, I paid more attention to the survivors' feelings than to theodicy or automatic ritual.

As I began to minister to families burying their loved ones and to witness their trials and traumas, I found myself concentrating on *feeling with them* more than on *explaining to them*. It was my undeclared personal bereavement joining in their bereavement. I recall an emotional resonance welling up from deep inside at every funeral, at every dedication, while I was speaking every memorial sermon as a rabbi.

I don't recall ever officiating as an unfeeling automaton. I never functioned as a ritual-reciter doing his job. While my body was standing at the pulpit or lectern, my heart was remembering and silently mourning. While I was the rabbi on the outside, I was the orphan on the inside.

This special ease in *feeling with* the mourners, a capability probably derived from my childhood and adolescent experiences, enabled me to relate to the mourners within my orbit on an intense pastoral level.

It appears to me that the wellspring of empathy and emotional involvement that stimulated me to develop the movement of Pastoral Bereavement Counseling during these past dozen years has its source in my personal experiences of loss and mourning that began 55 years ago.

Then came the active rabbinate. My professional service to my one and only congregation in New York City for almost 40 years provided an opportunity to experience hands-on contact with many others' tragedies and losses. During all those 40 years I *wanted* to help mourners but didn't know how. During the last 10 years I have been privileged to practice and teach a more effective way than in the first thirty.

HOW CLERGY RELATE TO MOURNERS

Clergy relate to mourners like everyone else—with fear and trepidation. Perhaps they'll lose some of their fear with experience, but sensitive clergy will never lose their sense of awe in touching the vital issues of life and death. Empathic clergy will feel spiritual tremors as they contemplate their intimate participation in the drama of love, loss, and hope that bereavement entails.

I remember my feelings as a young rabbi. I didn't sleep the night before the first funeral I was to perform for a congregant. I was frightened at the prospect of witnessing the family's pain and of feeling my own.

I had no idea of how I might meet the responsibility of leading the survivors through a difficult and painful hour—a task the family assumed I knew how to discharge. I was afraid I would make a mistake and appear to be unprofessional. My worst fear was that some error on my part would increase the family's sorrow.

I remember that I called an older colleague for advice. He was kind enough to advise me on the ritual aspects.

"Just follow the manual and you'll do fine. I usually change the sequence of the prayers slightly, but for the first time it would be easier to follow the pattern that's in the manual. Remember that the religious law is to complete the burial before reciting the kaddish. Be careful to follow the prescribed order for the burial ritual.

"Choose a text for the eulogy from the portion of the Torah Reading scheduled for the upcoming Sabbath synagogue services. If you like, I'll suggest an appropriate text. Review your notes from the Practical Rabbinics Course that you took at the Seminary."

But there was no hint of recognition of my troublesome emotions or of my concern for the feelings of the mourners. These things I would have to learn about from my own experiences. I would have to continue to experiment with how best to utilize empathy.

Contrary to what the lay public might expect, the seminaries that educate for the ministry devote little space in their curricula for preparing clergy to face the emotional overtones of their pastoral functions. I can understand some reasons—grief is a painful subject, and until now there did not exist a systematic self-contained method for helping mourners that could be effectively taught and applied.

I'm hoping that the establishment of our program in New York and the publication of this book, which is an effort at introducing and explaining our program, will help to fill that void.

But then, in my early rabbinate, there was no choice but to fall back upon my own devices. I recall that I began to experiment by adding personal nuances to the prescribed ritual. I began to interpret the standard prayers in a manner that would convey to the mourning survivors that I was *open to their feelings and thought it healthy for them to express them.* I tried to suggest that they might perceive this sorrowful event in their lives in a constructive perspective.

"Yes, a funeral is a painful and tragic happening, yes, it is a religious and solemn experience, but it is not a time for shutting yourselves off from natural feelings. It's perfectly normal and very healthy to be aware of your inner emotions and of their intensity."

I didn't know if other colleagues felt a similar call, but I felt it was correct and helpful to look for a better way than the prevailing rule. I thought it would prove to be healthy and beneficial, and the families I was serving seemed to agree. The word spread in the community that there was a young and sympathetic rabbi in Washington Heights who added a dimension of warmth and openness to the mechanics of a funeral service.

I will never forget a Wednesday morning in the early 1950s, the day before Thanksgiving. A few minutes after 10 o'clock a funeral director from the Bronx called to ask that I come to a funeral service scheduled for 2 o'clock that afternoon. (There were no burials possible for the next 3 days because of the holiday and the Sabbath, and Jewish law prescribes interment as soon as possible.)

"The family needs someone like you," he said. "This is a very tragic case, you have to know what happened. We'll be burying an eight-year-old boy who was playing in the street in front of his house, and was run over by a car. It happened just after 9 o'clock this morning—"

"You mean, about an hour ago? My God, and you're talking about a funeral for today?"

"We have to, you know, this is a holiday weekend coming up."

"My God, those poor parents, what's happening to them? Do they have any other children?"

"Yes, there's a ten-year-old brother that's left. It's tragic and shocking, the whole neighborhood is upset. Will you come?"

I said that I would and hung up the phone. My first thought was, "What am I going to say? How will I handle this? My God, that poor mother and father. This morning their little boy was alive, this afternoon they're going to bury him." My feelings were intensified by thoughts of how I would feel if something like this happened to our own three-year-old son.

What I said that afternoon was probably not as important as the sincerity of "feeling with" that needed to be conveyed. I remember that I desperately tried to demonstrate to the grieving parents that *everyone* was enveloped in a sense of utter and helpless sorrow.

I did this instinctively; but now I understand *why* it may have helped. Any preachment, any philosophy or canned wisdom would have been hopelessly out of place. If my presence there helped, it was because they saw my demeanor as a *validation* and *legitimization* of what they were dimly feeling. If it helped, it was on a nonrational primal level.

Presence, attitude, sincerity of sympathy, listening, openness to feelings, sharing of emotion, suggestion of hope and extending quiet support—these, I learned from that experience, are more helpful than attempts at explanation or high-sounding phrases.

Although they were not of my congregation, I maintained contact with that family during the weeks and months following the tragedy. Though I can't recall precisely, I must have offered them some of what I would now describe as informal unstructured counseling—spending time, listening, tuning in to their feeling, avoiding easy clichés, gently pointing to reasons for gratitude.

In time, another baby son was born, and I was invited to the older brother's bar mitzvah and wedding. This episode was, for me, a compelling demonstration of what an extra offering of empathy can do for a grieving family. It was part of the chain of significant experiences that led me to Pastoral Bereavement Counseling.

Other tragic situations arose, both within the congregational family and out of it. Sudden accidental deaths, lingering illnesses, heart attacks, malignancies, children's deaths, suicides—the whole range of misfortunes and calamities.

Over the years, the empathy that reverberated within me was translated into atypical approaches, different from what most of my colleagues employed. Instead of "words of comfort," which I found to be of limited value to most mourners, I activated a different approach.

I relied upon gentleness and sincerity towards the survivors, active listening, open sharing of whatever emotions were expressed or were not fully expressible. I was satisfied that what I was doing was genuinely helpful, and those I served in this manner seemed to agree.

Whenever possible, especially in cases of sudden tragedy, I would visit the family immediately upon hearing the news. Sometimes I could help in the funeral arrangements; but I found that of greater importance was "being there." Even sitting with silent empathy with a stricken survivor, giving them a chance to talk, or cry, or complain, or wail—is helpful. This can't be done hurriedly. The clergyperson must block out a specific amount of time and not feel pressured.

I added other personal touches. Even now, I never begin a funeral by walking briskly to the lectern. I stand for a few moments at the casket—deliberately and significantly. I allow myself to think a silent prayer that God may help me to conduct a proper prayer service, one that will give due dignity to the life of the deceased and provide a measure of comfort to the mourners. By now, this has become a gesture that permits everyone—myself included—to tune in to the emotional depths of the situation.

In the eulogy, I rarely speak only of the life and achievements of the person. I try to include some recognition of the family's feelings at this moment of saying good-bye, and of what they may be fearing to endure in the weeks ahead. I also include words of general faith, of courage and hope, but I point more to what I empathically imagine they're feeling at the moment.

I try not to appear "impressive," all-knowing, and all-wise. I try to project that we are all confronting together, as mortals, the mystery of life and death. I seek to be not above them, I try to take the posture of being one of them—which in fact I am.

During the years of serving as the rabbi of a congregation, I also developed the practice of informal follow-up of all my families in mourning. I would arrange a visit a month or so after the *shiva*—Jews observe the first week after the funeral as a period of regulated mourning—to spend a half hour in general conversation.

Usually, there were expressions of sadness and loneliness, to which I would respond with empathy and gentle support. Very often, mourners would add something along these lines: "But don't worry, Rabbi, I'll be all right. I'm strong, I'll manage, my sister managed when she lost her husband, I have many friends, thanks for coming."

I now understand that this was their way of expressing the stoicism that they thought society was expecting of them. I always offered to help if they wanted to see me again, but they rarely did—the same stoicism. I felt basically satisfied that I was doing my duty. I felt secretly pleased that such visits were enhancing my reputation in the community and contributed to goodwill for my congregation.

This was the extent of my pastoral service to mourners, aside from fulfilling the continuous religious and ritual requirements that I and my staff performed. I honestly thought I was completely meeting my responsibilities—perhaps even adding a little extra. To the best of my knowledge, these were the parameters within which all empathic clergy served bereaved people. I didn't know of anyone who was doing more. I was there when people needed me, I gave of my time and expended my emotional energy without stint and with skill, I was doing my job.

It never dawned upon me, during 30 active years of service to thousands of mourners, that there was an undiscovered universe of pain and emotional distress *in which all mourners are submerged*. Some mourners are aware of what they are enduring. Some are in even greater pain, because they and the world around them *deny* that there is such a hell.

It should not have taken so long. During all those years, I should have earlier perceived that *clergy could become the ideal community resource to facilitate a mourner's passage through that region*. I did not realize during my first 30 years that with all the earnest feeling and sincerity at my disposal and with all the skill that I could muster, I was failing to provide for mourners what they urgently needed and were not receiving.

I did not understand—I didn't even suspect—that bereavement plunges a mourner into the depths of an ocean of painful emotions. What I had been dealing with for 30 years, what most clergy deal with in their blissful ignorance, are the surface ripples of these emotions. But mourners are battered by violent currents that surge beneath; it isn't enough to throw them a life preserver on the surface.

Pastoral Bereavement Counseling is an effort to suggest to clergy, "You would be doing God's work if you learned how to dive down *with the mourners* to the region of their pain beneath the surface and help them return to the top." We believe we can show you a way to do this effectively and safely.

THE MIRACLE OF STRUCTURED COUNSELING

The next fortuitous turn of my life put me on the final leg of the path that led to the development of a systematic method to heal the wounds of the bereaved.

In 1972 I received a Masters degree in Pastoral Counseling from Iona College, and completed 2 years of supervised counseling experiences at the Jewish Family Service of New York.

I was continuing my rabbinic work at the Fort Tryon Jewish Center and serving as the Jewish Chaplain at St. Clare's, a major Catholic Hospital; I also began to use my newly acquired skills as a Pastoral Counselor, setting up structured counseling sessions for people needing help in a variety of situations. Cases of marital discord, one instance of promiscuity, depression, and aftermath of divorce, came to my attention.

I felt great satisfaction in setting up and carrying through counseling in a definite structure—not informally, as I had done in years past. It was a new method in the arsenal of approaches to trying to help people. It seemed to be a useful mechanism for creating a focus of attention on a specific need, and provided an effective frame for a therapeutic transaction.

As I saw it, it made possible the harnessing of both heart and mind for a sacred purpose. It blended empathy and technical skill. I found it very satisfying to be able to apply a combination of my emotional and intellectual energies to the solution of someone's problem.

Recently bereaved people were continuing to come to me for informal sessions. On one occasion, one of these informal bereavement sessions happened to be sandwiched between two formal hour-long appointments. As I glanced at that page in my date book, the seed of a new idea was suddenly planted.

Why not schedule a widow for a full hour? Shouldn't I regard her experience of inner pain with the same earnestness and from a similar professional perspective with which I do structured therapy? Why should mourning deserve less expertise than any other life crisis?

I realized that I would be venturing into uncharted waters. No colleague I knew was offering structured counseling to mourners. In fact, very few were extending even informal ministrations. But I also sensed an extraordinary opportunity for an extension of empathic skills into a field that could benefit unlimited numbers of people. I began to consider the idea seriously.

There were certain definite counseling problems to consider. How do you set up this therapeutic transaction? How do you begin? When and how do you conclude? What might the goals and expectations be—for the client and for the counselor? What special techniques might be applicable?

I sensed that there might be a need to prevent a buildup of client dependence upon the counselor due to the intensity of a mourner-client's special need for support in the aftermath of a loss. Conversely, I myself might be tied up in emotional knots because of possible stirring up of my own memories and experiences.

What do I do if I get into deep water? Can I undertake this without a backup system? What criteria determine whether a mourner requires more intensive therapy than I can provide? To whom can I refer a mourner should the need arise?

It is now 12 years later, and this book undertakes to describe the system that we have instituted to safeguard all these concerns. Needless to say, it has taken more time than I ever expected, but the results of the program to date and the potential benefits that will accrue in the wake of further expansion make our efforts eminently worthwhile.

We received initial financial grants from the United Hospital Fund of Greater New York, and from the Federation of Jewish Philanthropies. We are very grateful for the guidance, encouragement, and cooperation we received from the New York Board of Rabbis and many other agencies and individuals. We are hopeful that with wider interest and participation the program will be able to be instituted nationally and funded on a self-sustaining basis.

The beginnings of some answers to the initial questions began to take shape after a year of tentative experimentation. I well remember the breakthrough case of the widow who improved dramatically after just five sessions.

Gertrude was the sister of a rabbinic colleague who called me in desperation to ask for help.

"Jack, I can't handle it, her sorrow and her constant crying," he said. "She's falling apart and I'm concerned for her. I don't know how to help. I'm grieving for my brother-in-law myself, and I don't know what to do. I've heard that you're available for this. What should I do?"

Her husband had died suddenly, she was left with two children, she couldn't cope. I felt the stirrings of empathy, even over the phone. Did my heart go out to her, sight unseen, because my heart remembered my mother losing my father? Was I perhaps feeling an echo of my own family sorrow?

I was on vacation, but I didn't hesitate to interrupt it and made an appointment. In hindsight, perhaps that was one of the keys to the subsequent successful intervention. I had already made an immediate emotional investment, prior to the first meeting. My empathy had already been engaged.

Gertrude came into my office highly agitated. I remember that she didn't even sit down for 20 minutes. A torrent of sorrow, anger, and hopelessness poured forth.

"What did I come for? You won't be able to help me, no one will be able to help. God did this to me, my life is over. What will happen to my children, our business is going to ruin, I can't think straight. I have no peace, I can't go on without him, I can't believe what's happened, there is no God, there is no justice, there's no meaning to anything. We were just beginning to get on our feet [they had both survived the Holocaust], and now it's all over.

"I'll never believe in God again, I won't fast on Yom Kippur. Leave me alone, don't talk to me. I'm wasting your time, I'm wasting my time, it won't do any good. My God, I don't know where to go."

I remember hearing those words and feeling her despair. I wanted to *let her know* that I felt her agony, but wasn't sure how to do it convincingly. I remember that I said a silent prayer: "Dear God, help me to help her. Let me think about it, what would be a helpful procedure? In this situation, how can I begin a therapeutic process? What technique shall I try? Listen to her, be empathic, feel with her, but also, think!—use your brain, use your intellect, choose an approach, don't give up—think!"

The effort at disciplining myself *to feel and think at the same* *time* turned out to be an important step. I was helped by remembering a phrase used by Harry Stack Sullivan in summarizing his theory of Interpersonal Psychiatry: "Be a Participant-Observer." In my mind, I interpreted it in shortcut fashion: "Use your feelings and intellect at the same time."*

Hesitantly, I began to use the counseling technique of "reflection," and after about 20 minutes her fever of agitation diminished somewhat. She began to notice my empathy and began to listen to my words. After a few more moments, she tentatively sat down on the edge of the seat. I silently thanked God and proceeded with the techniques I had decided to use.

By the end of the first hour, it was clear that we had moved towards a helpful therapeutic relationship and that the counseling sessions would proceed. From that point on, we both sensed the unfolding of a miracle. Her journeying through the natural sequences of emotions in the bereavement process was so rapid (unusual in the light of my later experiences), that we were able to terminate after four more meetings.

I recall that when Gertrude said good-bye and left my office, I sensed that this had been, at least for me, trail blazing therapy. I spent two intensive hours reviewing my notes and outlining the counseling exchanges that had flowed between us. I remember being excited as I discerned the emergence of a definite pattern that could have accounted for our apparent success.

My review pointed towards a particular approach and to certain techniques that seemed to have been very effective. I began to suspect then that our success in this instance had not been accidental, but that it was the result of the application of specific counseling skills in a particularly appropriate way.

---

*This is not an exact use of Interpersonal Psychiatric *theory*. I was only adapting a phrase.

Sullivan's approach emphasizes that the therapist should be aware that his own feelings *always* bear upon the therapeutic situation, that the therapist should at least be aware of that factor, and at best, seek to use it actively in the therapeutic exchange. In this instance the phrase was used as a reminder and a spur to self-discipline in seeking a solution to a clinical difficulty.

I didn't fully realize it at the time, but this experience was actually the beginning of the formulation of the theory of Pastoral Bereavement Counseling.

In this chapter, I have tried to present an account of how Pastoral Bereavement Counseling evolved. As I see it, three main factors were involved—my early bereavements, a lifelong career in the rabbinate, and years of experimentation that have led to the discovery of a specific system of grief counseling.

Our program recommends that clergy be trained to choose certain clearly defined counseling skills to be utilized within the framework of a specially designed therapeutic structure, with the goal of bringing healing to the mourner's wounds.

In the last 10 years, the original tentative experiments have evolved into a completely articulated program that has been successfully established in New York. We have reason to believe that the principles and techniques are valid and appropriate, that they can be identified and taught to all clergy (and others) who may be interested. We are now in a position to extend this program into other communities.

Chapter 2

WHY A BETTER WAY IS NEEDED

I remember my frustrations as I recognized the inherent inadequacies of my unstructured ministrations to mourners. I would have been grateful to anyone who would have been able to teach me a better way.

I remember searching for more effective means, not accepting my dissatisfaction. I felt a need to light at least a small candle in a corner of the great darkness that exists for most mourners.

I soon found that I was venturing into new terrain. It seemed that everyone was skirting the subject, dealing with "mourning" in general, but showing little concern for mourners in the flesh. The research projects that I was aware of were valuable and important but made no pretense of directly easing the plight of the actual mourner.

I attended many seminars and listened to experts at many conferences, workshops, and symposia, but found no applicable or useful answer. I heard no one recommending specific counseling techniques to employ in dealing with mourners. There were hardly any explorations, even on a tentative basis, attempting to formulate a philosophy that might encourage clergy—or anyone else, for that matter—to answer the cry that the bereaved silently shriek.

I found many people talking *about* bereavement but very few undertaking to *directly help mourners*. Seminars were announced on the theme of "Grief and Mourning" but avoided a clear focusing on the area of bereavement per se. Even those few programs that included *some* descriptions of a mourner's feelings and *some* description of how to alleviate their deep trauma, treated the subject in a peripheral and incomplete manner.

Many people were talking about Death and Dying, but I saw almost no one targeting *delivery of actual and effective support.* It reminded me of the commonplace about the weather—"Everyone talks about it, but no one does anything about it."

I knew from my own experience and that of my colleagues—clergy of all denominations—that the religious Establishment had not devised or experimented with any model for relating to mourners in a structured way. The best that could be said about our traditional ways of offering consolation—preachment, philosophy, advice-giving, explaining or defending God's acts—was that they were well-meaning and well-intentioned.

Perhaps they had been effective in a God-oriented culture; but they were less useful for most mourners today. If we think about it, we might even understand that preachment, advice-giving, and explaining God is often more of a response to the clergyperson's needs than to the mourner's. Such approaches today are at best irrelevant; at worst they can damage a mourner's emotional health.

Pastoral Bereavement Counseling is not only effective for the mourner who needs it, it can also be inspiring for the counselor who practices it. Pastoral Bereavement Counseling is a method that derives from a religious orientation; it is a fulfillment of a religious commandment. It is not only a genuine service to man, it is an act that is pleasing to God. Therein lies its potential power. It combines a *benefit for the mourner* with a *spiritual reward for the counselor.*

A PLEA—NOT CENSURE

These words of criticism are not meant to be a wholesale judgment of *all* clergy, or of *all* community mental health agencies, or of *every* health professional. Many are deeply concerned with the problem and are doing what they can. But we believe that there should and could be larger numbers and deeper commitment.

Over the years, I have become acquainted with several clergy who are especially sensitive to the needs of the bereaved. They have searched for ways to infuse their ministry to mourners with a sense of genuine love and concern. Several hospital chaplains have demonstrated exceptional skill in transmitting their deep empathy to bereaved families.

Yet, all of us together form only a tiny nucleus, we are voices in the wilderness. At best, we are isolated individuals struggling to make ourselves more perfect instruments of God's compassion. If we could form ourselves into a movement, we could transform our individual empathies into a galvanizing force. We would be able to bring healing to many mourners, not just a few. This is the ultimate purpose of the movement that we call Pastoral Bereavement Counseling.

By presenting a summary model of our experiences, we hope to promote a fourfold consciousness:

> That mourners legitimately need help in facing their perplexities and pain;
>
> That too few nonmourners (those who are not actively mourning a specific loss at a given moment) have been able or willing to provide such help in a freely accessible manner;
>
> That our movement offers a method that can make accessible such effective support;
>
> That those who volunteer to join our movement will know that they are serving man and feel that they are pleasing God.

A Few Who Try to Help

Among nonclergy mental health professionals—social workers, psychiatrists, nurses—and among administrators of hospitals and hospices, family counseling services and community health clinics, there is a growing interest in setting up Bereavement Care programs. National and local organizations have established mutual support programs, opportunities for rap sessions, widow-to-widow networks, hotline facilities. They have distributed newsletters, pamphlets, and magazines. They have provided facilities where recently bereaved persons can share feelings, exchange advice, and participate in social and cultural activities.

Obviously, our movement of Pastoral Bereavement Counseling cannot claim to be the only one in the field. There are many others engaged in significant and worthwhile activity. But we see some unique features in our program that we believe give it great potential.

Our program allows for greater engagement with a mourner's intense subterranean emotions than may be touched by attendance at group sessions or other follow-up activities. Because it is a religion-related activity, we can offer bereavement counseling with less stigma of "needing help," and with no need to charge fees.

We believe that our movement can create a more natural and legitimate atmosphere in the mourner's environment where there will be less need to overcome the feeling, "There must be something wrong with me if I can't handle it myself." Ultimately, we hope to deliver healing help to many mourners who are presently, in effect, being abandoned to their own devices.

We suggest that our readers might consider the role they may come to play in this developing ministry of healing, whether they are clergy or not. We will need many hands and many caring people.

THE NINE UNIQUE FEATURES OF PASTORAL BEREAVEMENT COUNSELING

We believe that Pastoral Bereavement Counseling is the better way because of nine special features.

1. It Recognizes the Heart of the Problem

Present methods give insufficient recognition and diluted attention to the heart of the bereavement crisis. By its very nature, the group process diffuses a needed concentration on the radical emotional and spiritual turbulence *that each mourner feels and each mourner must pass through.*

The only sure way towards healing grief is to guide the mourner *through that turbulence.* Pastoral Bereavement Counselors seek to do this with deliberate intention and with charity aforethought. We approach this task armed with a premeditated design.

As far as we can perceive, the methods presently being used in programs of bereavement care are—even when they succeed in reaching their stated goals—only an introduction to those intense feelings, seldom a sustained immersion.

2. It Emphasizes Empathy as a Principal Therapeutic Tool

Our experience with counseling hundreds of mourners has convinced us of the indispensability of empathy in successful Pastoral Bereavement Counseling.

The counselor's sensitivity to the mourner's pain is the essential ingredient in the motivation that brings him to this enterprise. The reverberations of his empathy throughout the course of the counseling, echoing the mourner's plight, sustain him in the difficult process of encouraging his client to face his pain without fleeing.

Each of the 10 techniques that will be recommended for use by Pastoral Bereavement Counselors will need to be applied with evident love, sincere concern, and palpable empathy. If the mourner doesn't "know" that the counselor is feeling emotions akin to what he himself is experiencing, the therapeutic results will be incomplete.

The philosophy and dynamic theory of Pastoral Bereavement Counseling, as will be detailed in subsequent chapters, places a greater premium on the importance of empathy than do other approaches to bereavement therapy. In our approach it is never a matter of technical skill only. It is always necessary to apply technique with feeling.

A cardinal rule for our counselors is—always allow yourself to be emotionally involved. Never face the mourner with detachment or in a casual manner. Always remember in your mind and heart that you are dealing with someone's deepest concerns, with primal anguish.

3. It Presents the Counselor as a Shepherd, Rather Than as a Technician

This perception can be a crucial factor in motivating the mourner to avail himself of the program that we offer, and in sustaining him to complete the counseling sessions.

Pastoral Bereavement Counseling is more pastoral than professional. It is designed to present the counselor to the mourner's consciousness as a shepherd who cares deeply about each member of his flock. For mourners who feel helpless, abandoned, and unloved, this can be extremely reassuring. It can be of great value in and of itself.

Pastoral Bereavement Counseling is derived from a distinctly religious orientation. The counselor's desire to serve God permeates the entire therapeutic exchange. Part of the spiritual and therapeutic power of the experience, felt by both client and counselor, arises from their simultaneous perception that a Higher Presence is conjoined with them in this particular exercise.

Ideally, our counselors will be motivated by hopes of achieving two sacred purposes. One is to help a human being—a "child of God"—who is in distress. Another is to fulfill a yearning to perform a religious deed that will find favor in God's eyes.

In the practice of Pastoral Bereavement Counseling our counselors are neither technicians nor professionals—therefore, they charge no fees. Their principal reward is the fulfillment of a religious commandment.

4. It Places an Essentially Religious Experience into an Essentially Religious Framework

Pastoral Bereavement Counseling conforms more closely to the religious searching that mourners experience than is possible with any other counseling mode. This is due to the spiritual nature of the mourner's feelings in being bereaved, and to the quasi-religious quality of the counseling experience.

The experience of facing the stark reality of death thrusts the mourner, in the most direct manner possible, into the maelstrom of life's awesome mystery. Confronting and contemplating the core questions of "Why death?" and "What is the meaning of life?" has been the stuff of religion for all ages. The personal experience that most moves us to wonder about the ultimate meaning of life and to ponder the question of what God wants of us, is the loss of a loved one.

At such a time it is more natural for the mourner to relate to a "religious" or "pastoral" figure than to a doctor or social worker or psychiatrist. At such a time, the local clergy figure may be the one resource to which the bereaved might instinctively respond, *if* the accessible clergyperson would prepare himself to genuinely respond to the mourner's needs.

In the performance of Pastoral Bereavement Counseling our counselors are engaged in intense religious activity. They are allowing their deep emotions to interact with the deep emotions of another human being—an equal child of God.

A session of Pastoral Bereavement Counseling can become suffused with a religious atmosphere, with sorrow and struggle intermingled with hope and prayer. These deep emotions can be felt and shared by client and counselor alike, at times reaching a point where they can feel themselves as a congregation-of-two. At such times the therapeutic process can approach an electricity and incandescence akin to religious fervor.

Pastoral Bereavement Counseling can become an extraordinary prayer to God, the obverse of liturgical worship. Congregational worship begins with words and progresses to feelings—bereavement counseling begins with feelings and moves to words. In bereavement counseling the process of grappling with elemental feelings and struggling to formulate and confront them honestly engages both mourner and counselor in a significant religious exercise.

Both public prayer and private bereavement counseling deal with mortal man reaching towards the immortal God. Both are concerned with the same sum of materials, albeit approached from different angles. When sincerity and concentration are present in both situations, who is to say which is higher!

5. It Legitimizes the Struggle with Religious Themes as Part of the Struggle with Grief

Pastoral Bereavement Counseling, as no other mode of support for the mourner, directly addresses the latent religious conflict which is at the heart of the mourner's perplexity. Part of a bereaved person's spiritual trauma is to accommodate the rage to rebel with the need to retain faith.

We are all mortals seeking to understand God's ways while our very mortality constricts us to mute our challenge. We need to understand; we need equally to accept that we will never fully understand. Job's classic cry, "Though You slay me, yet I believe in You," expresses the conflict pithily. The unspoken dilemma of grief is: "How can I be angry—but not too much—at God?"

On the one hand, the mourner is forced to confront the injustice of the fates. His anger may extend so far as to tempt him, in his imagination, even to challenge God. Yet at the same moment, he feels a great need for spiritual reassurance. He feels a compulsion to believe that God has not utterly abandoned him.

It is not unusual to rage against the fates and at the same time to be grateful for a portion of good fortune. It is human to feel sadness—and/or anger—at the curtailment of our beloved's existence, and at the same time revel in the sensation of the preciousness of our own.

This psycho-spiritual predicament is a dimension of the grief process that is beyond—or at least additional to—the accepted scope of therapeutic attention. It is, in a manner of speaking, *meta*-therapeutic. Yet, the need to address this dimension—or at least to recognize it as an important factor in mourning—has been largely absent in our approaches to mourning up to now.

Pastoral Bereavement Counseling includes this factor in the list of the mourner's treatable concerns, and on the agenda of the counselor's program of support. We see our awareness of and our attention to this factor as part of the uniqueness of our approach.

6. *Pastoral Bereavement Counseling Is More Than an Inch Deep*

Pastoral Bereavement Counselors aim to "walk with" the mourner—to become his personal companion—as he descends into the stages of deep torment and pain. Pastoral Bereavement Counselors aim to "swim with" the mourner as he feels himself drowning in an ocean of despair. This is our specific intent, and constitutes the reason for our program's special design.

Whereas other approaches seem to be content with attention to the mourner's surface and visible difficulties, our program postulates that the only way to effectively help is to consciously chart a course that will navigate the mourner through his subterranean emotional currents. We believe that the only genuine course is "diving deep."

To the best of our knowledge, we are the only mental health practitioners that deliberately design a course that will take both us and our clients into an awareness of deep pain. The mourner must become aware of his pain because this is the only route to healing—the sharper the clarity of his awareness, the sooner and more wholesome his recovery. The counselor needs to be aware of his pain, for only then will he be able to bring honest empathy to bear upon the situation. Without honest empathy he will not be perceived as an honest-to-goodness companion.

To the best of our knowledge, we are the only mental health practitioners who welcome being troubled by the mourner's troubled feelings. The counselor's demonstration of not flinching from feeling pain silently encourages the mourner to take the same path. By providing this example in his own flesh the counselor seems to be saying to the mourner, "Follow me as we pass through your troubled feelings, which are mine, too."

For those who want to heal the mourner's deep pain, we see no other way. Surface treatment of deep pain is not only ineffective, it can strike the mourner as callous and insensitive.

We are suggesting that Pastoral Bereavement Counselors take as their open and declared goal the mission to accompany the mourner in the tasting, experiencing, and working through of their powerful emotions. Working towards that goal will be more helpful to the mourner than choosing a treatment that is well-intentioned but only skin-deep.

In contrast, to the best of our knowledge and understanding, the bereavement programs presently available in the United States have accepted more modest goals. To the best of our knowledge, they themselves describe their aims and purposes along these lines:

> To give mourners an opportunity to ventilate some of their feelings;
>
> To give mourners an opportunity of witnessing that others have similar distress;
>
> To impart some knowledge about the normal course of bereavement;
>
> To extend some practical coping advice;
>
> To provide some opportunities for social and cultural activities.*

---

*The volume, *Bereavement: Reactions, Consequences and Care,* National Academic Press, 1984, a 295-page report on the state of the art by a committee appointed by the Institute of Medicine at the invitation of the Office of Prevention of the National Institute of Mental Health, describes the aims of hospice bereavement programs as follows: "Although about 70 percent of hospices offer services for about a year following bereavement, these efforts are modest. Such services may include home visits, phone calls, letters, social gathers, support groups, counseling, anniversary remembrances, and referral to other support services.

"Like mutual support services, hospices emphasize education and support.

"The goals of follow-up bereavement services are: to provide family members with information about the normal grief process; to provide grieving family members an opportunity to review and reflect on the experience of caring for their loved ones and their loss experience; to assess and monitor individual coping ability, stress levels, and available support; to encourage family members to utilize existing support systems or to seek and create additional sources of support.

"Although some hospices offer limited psychotherapeutic counseling, most do not." (pp. 251–252)

These activities are undoubtedly of some value and better than no efforts at all; yet they are surface applications that only go skin-deep. What would be more helpful and of greater value would be an open and direct commitment to participate with the mourner in the depth and intensity of his grief. This is what Pastoral Bereavement Counselors aim to do.

Similarly, we regard the traditional ministerial efforts to "console and comfort" mourners by words of wisdom, philosophy, or faith as being of limited value and only short-term usefulness. We do not perceive these efforts as going to the "heart of the matter."

"Comfort and consolation" do little more to bring genuine healing to the mourner than a sedative does to heal a heart attack. It may temporarily alleviate the pain, but totally ignores the causes and may interfere with the optimum course of treatment.

It seems to us that traditional ministerial efforts in this area have accomplished little more than satisfying the clergyperson's ego and lulling the mourner into believing that someone cares. The mourner's needs—his deep emotional traumas—haven't even been noticed.

Pastoral Bereavement Counseling can show the way to notice and can teach a way to heal. We aim, first, to enunciate a counseling approach that is consonant with the theoretical dynamics of grief and that appropriately relates to the actual words and feelings of mourners. We will cite those words and feelings from the hundreds of case histories in our files.

We aim, second, to establish a system of community bereavement counseling that would enable delivery of effective healing services to all mourners in the community. We believe this could go a long way toward meeting the emotional needs of many mourners who presently feel abandoned.

7. Pastoral Bereavement Counseling Utilizes a Community Resource That Has Been Underemployed Till Now

Our program cannot be instituted by the clergy alone. It is hoped that they will undertake to learn the counseling skills required and agree to provide the counseling under responsible clinical supervision. But they will not be able, in most instances, to organize the whole program and to establish it in the community.

The community leadership—business, institutional, and health agencies—will need to provide the coordinating and record-keeping office, the advertising and outreach activities, the public approbation of all the participants, and the vision, the determination, and the initiative to launch the project.

But the clergy of the community—for all denominations—are in the ideal position to furnish the volunteer manpower to perform most of the counseling. It is within their province, as shepherds of their flocks, and as facilitators of the difficult process of helping people to deal with God's ways, to undertake this task.

We are certain that many clergy, at some points in their ministries, have sincerely wanted to help mourners. Perhaps, in the absence of a systematic and approved method, they may have allowed this desire to wane. We are hoping that the arrival on the scene of Pastoral Bereavement Counseling, with its potential for benefiting all concerned, will rekindle a spark of motivation for many clergy to serve in this area.

We believe that the optimum way to effective help for mourners is through one-to-one counseling rather than through group sharing. Individual mourners move through the grief journey at different speeds and paces, and the group process cannot provide the empathic attention that individuals may need *at their own stages.*

How could we recruit the large number of volunteer counselors to serve the large number of needy mourners? The only potential reservoir for such a large number is the corps of clergy and ministers who are already serving congregations in their communities. Our program is an effort to recruit numbers from this corps of clergy, to harness their latent energy and interest, and to implement this crucially needed service in a constructive and responsible manner.

Our experience indicates that with the involvement of caring individuals, and with the collaboration of hospitals and community counseling agencies, clergy will be enabled to provide this much-needed service to their communities.

8. More Mourners Will Come Forth for Help Because Pastoral Bereavement Counselors Accept No Fee from the Client

This is an essential component of our program's appeal to the mourner. We ask our counselors to contribute their skills to the service of their fellow mortals, without compensation, for altruistic reasons—to help their fellowman—and for religious reasons—to please God. But the rationale for the "no fee" goes much deeper, and makes this an indispensable feature in our overall design.

To the best of our knowledge, we are the only mental health practitioners who offer our services without charge. We do so, first, in order to *test the authenticity* of the sense of compassion that must be recognized as a principal motivation in our decision to become bereavement counselors.

It is this compassion, when we succeed in tuning it up to a high and steady pitch, that makes it possible for us to counsel effectively. Without this embracing compassion it would not be possible for us to perform our task of almost literally walking hand in hand with the mourner who is entering the valley of the shadow of grief.

Second, Pastoral Bereavement Counselors who would ask for a fee would place in doubt the mourner's certainty that the counselor loves him. Questions would arise as to whether the counselor is truly willing or able to share the load of grief, or if he is a true shepherd. Even a twinge of dim resentment can interfere with the therapeutic efficacy of any intervention.

The nature of the empathic exchange in bereavement counseling is so subtle and fragile as to be easily spoiled, even by a request that can be rationally defended. At a time of mourning for a significant past love, the mourner can be healed only by feeling himself the recipient of unconditional and unearned love. If we were to ask for a fee, the mourner might be further damaged by his suspicion that a budding source of comfort is withdrawing from him.

The stakes are too high to run an unnecessary risk. The entire exercise can be jeopardized by an injudicious request. The mourner whom we wish to serve is entitled to the protection of feeling that the counselor's motives are entirely pure and untainted.

Third, asking for a fee would create an additional impediment at a moment when mourners are wavering and pondering whether to apply for help. The mourner's consumption of emotional energy to overcome the built-in resistances to accepting an offer of help—fear of opening himself to another, fear of his future, fear of facing his vague and indescribable torments—is sufficiently draining and difficult in itself. We should avoid placing an additional strain upon him.

Of course a fee is defensible and reasonable. But if our genuine aim—as shepherds—is to encourage those who could use help to accept it, it appears inappropriate to charge a fee.

We are aware of the counterargument—that requiring a fee is a test of the applicant's genuine need and readiness for counseling. But this argument is less compelling in the case of mourners, whose presenting problems are in no way attributable to their own actions, than from those suffering from stresses traceable to their own personality or life-styles.

9. Pastoral Bereavement Counseling Removes the Stigma of "Needing Help" That Has Prevented Many Mourners from Seeking and Accepting It

Nonmourners and society in general have unwittingly increased the mourner's burden by telegraphing the feeling to grieving people that they are basically on their own. "Be strong!" is the message many mourners pick up from friends and strangers alike. "You'll be able to manage, everyone does, be stoic, put up a brave front, nobody wants to see you crying, laugh and the world laughs with you, cry and you'll cry alone."

We will never be able to assess the mental health damage that was inflicted on millions of Americans who have suffered bereavement since 1963, when President John F. Kennedy was assassinated. The portrayal of perfect stoicism, the hiding of elemental emotions at a time of intense anguish, confirmed the notion for millions that it is proper for mourners to stifle feelings.

The picture of courage and manliness—"Don't shed a tear"—that was engraved on the national consciousness that fateful weekend was, from the point of view of ensuring mental health, the worst possible subliminal message that could have been conveyed. It has become clearer during the last two decades that depressed, avoided, or insufficiently confronted emotions can only hurt mental wholesomeness.

It is becoming clearer every year that mourners who, consciously or not, inhibit their personal grieving process, are at higher risk for somatic and mental distress than those who acknowledge their grief and who allow themselves to journey through their emotional stages.

Repression is a temporary Band-Aid that allows the sore to fester; expression is a soft balm that allows the wound to heal.

Clearly, our national and cultural tragedy is that the ideal of stoicism prevents many mourners from availing themselves of even the minimum support services that are available. For many there has been erected a silent psychological barrier: "Be a man, don't ask for help, it's an admission of weakness."

Consciously or not, the prevailing operative notion in many mourners' minds is, "I don't want to go to a widows' or widowers' meeting, I don't want to be seen as needing someone else's support, it will only make me feel inferior."

Our experience in New York has indicated that this barrier is lowered, if not completely overcome, by the helper being a clergyperson, who is seen in our society as a traditional helping figure. More often than not, a religious figure is the one called upon to officiate at the funeral, and the one who offers some measure of post-funeral consolation. In the public mind, those activities have been regarded as part of their duty and function.

From the mourner's point of view, therefore, and especially where there will be public endorsement and local involvement in the establishment of a Pastoral Bereavement Counseling Program, it can be less threatening to turn to a clergyperson for help. It can appear to be more normal than turning to a psychiatrist, social worker, agency, or any professional practitioner.

These professionals and community agencies have an indispensable partnership role to play in establishing and maintaining a Pastoral Bereavement Counseling program. They are needed in the clinical supervision process, and to provide intensive therapy in individual cases where indicated.

But the clergy in any community immediately become the

first-line resource for mourners as soon as the community begins to consider the possibility of introducing our program. Bereavement counseling is a preventive mental health service that will need a tremendous number of dedicated volunteers.

We believe that the local clergy will turn out to be the ideal candidates for this task. By their previous training and practical experience, by their lifelong interests and dedication to service, by virtue of the leadership position they occupy in their community, by the innate relationship of empathy with their role as pastors in the public mind, the clergy can be the largest reservoir of potential counselors for our movement.

They will need supplementary training to prepare them for their tasks, and clinical supervision to become proficient. But they are our primary hope for the expansion of our project.

For all of these reasons, we believe that Pastoral Bereavement Counseling is a better way for clergy and the community to support its mourners than has been employed till now. We regard it as a new frontier in mental health activity which needs to be explored fully and without delay. We have seen it to be beneficial to mourners and counselors, and believe it will be a blessing for every community in which it will be established.

The next chapters will present a model of the dynamic features of Pastoral Bereavement Counseling—the rationale of its design, the theory and application of its recommended counseling techniques, and the practical steps necessary to introduce it into American communities.

Chapter 3

PASTORAL BEREAVEMENT COUNSELING—WHAT IT IS

Pastoral Bereavement Counseling is a series of eight conversations between a bereaved person and the one who wishes to help him. The words that are spoken are usually heavily freighted with emotion, pain, and hope. The helper's reactions are never random or thoughtless, they are always directed towards reaching a definable therapeutic goal.

Much more than conversation takes place. There is a sharing of feeling as the counselor witnesses the mourner struggling to find healing. There is the sharing of feeling as the mourner witnesses the counselor's sincerity and empathy.

The counselor feels the course of his empathy throughout the entire course of the counseling. He is aware of his own pervasive struggle—mental and emotional—to choose the most effective approach. At every moment of the sessions the counselor is weighing alternative strategies—through words, attitude, suggestions, silences, and combinations thereof—to try to select the best course.

A Different Posture Towards Helping Mourners

A Pastoral Bereavement Counseling session is not an ordinary conversation. It is unusually intense and palpably significant. It is both therapy and prayer, and equally so for both mourner and counselor. For both principals it is a process of yearning and learning.

For the mourner it is a life experience that aims to assuage—in some significant measure—his sense of bottomless tragedy. For the counselor it is a potential fulfillment—in the most genuine manner possible—of a deeply felt wish to help a fellow mortal with more than platitudes.

The eight conversations are imbued with the perception, on the part of both the counselor and counselee, that they are together engaged in a significant journey that must inevitably affect both of them.

The bereaved are seeking a specific answer for their particular pain at this juncture in their lives. The counselor has an opportunity to genuinely serve both God and man, and to creatively confront his own sense of mystery about life and death.

Both need to open themselves to whatever thoughts and feelings may arise in their consciousness during the 8-week exercise. Both need to open themselves to the possibility of an experience, a turning of a corner, that will have immediate as well as lifelong consequences. Both are serving God by grappling with life's problems with vigor and intensity, each at a particular juncture in their lives.

Both together have become partners with God during this activity—infinitesimal partners, but filling roles that are not utterly insignificant. True, the quantity of our mortal presence in this aspect of the God-man relationship is very tiny. But the quality of our presence, the question of how human existence relates to God's overall purpose, may be highly significant.

There's reason to believe that God does need us—otherwise, He would heal mourners entirely without us. What He seems to be saying to us is, "I'm sorry, but the only way to heal a mourner's pain is to let him struggle with it. If you struggle with the mourner through that journey of pain, you're helping him and Me."

This sense of engaging in an activity that is clearly in the "here and now" and yet also touches the mystery of eternity can insert a palpable religious dimension into a conversation or a therapeutic session. This infusion of a transcendental quality into a practical program makes this activity appropriate as part of a pastoral ministry. Pastoral Bereavement Counseling is a vehicle through which a shepherd responds to God's command to serve both the Master and the flock.

We recognize that there may be others besides clergy, who are mental health practitioners or in allied fields, who might feel themselves called to be shepherds or pastors to mourners. While our principal intention is to recruit bereavement counselors from the ranks of the clergy, we can now envision that others also will feel impelled to participate with us. We hope that everyone who joins will find deep satisfaction in their work. We hope they will come to see themselves as blessed instruments of God's healing.

Pastoral Bereavement Counselors will be asked to dedicate their mental, emotional, and spiritual skills for one hour each week to the service of healing a mourner. We ask them to make this contribution as a freewill offering to help a human being who is in pain. At the same time they will be performing a religious deed, an act that we believe is commanded by God, and that we believe is pleasing to Him.

We ask them to do this *for the other* without fee or compensation. For the sacrifice of their time and the sadness that will singe their lives as a consequence of their freely sharing *the other's* pain, we hope they will be rewarded with emotional and spiritual satisfaction. We pray that they will often succeed and many times attain a peak sense of genuine fulfillment.

SEVEN ATTITUDES THAT MAKE IT POSSIBLE

A Pastoral Bereavement Counselor will need to develop a new inner orientation to the process of preparing for his mission. His effectiveness will depend on whether he adopts a different framework of postures and attitudes in relating to others than he may have previously employed.

We suggest to you the following new attitudinal requirements:

1. Be clear about your motives.
2. Understand and subscribe to the ethos of our program's overall design and structure.
3. Intensify your initial surface empathy to allow your feelings to resonate deeply with the mourner's actual pain.
4. Understand the dynamics of the recommended counseling skills, and seek to apply them competently and consistently.
5. Increase the efficacy of your empathy and counseling skills by consciously connecting them to a specific and attainable goal, and by never losing sight of that connection.
6. Understand that goal-directed empathy requires patience, tolerance, acceptance, and love.
7. Look forward to the possibility of bereavement counseling becoming—at certain times and under certain circumstances—a deep religious experience for yourself and for the mourner.

Each of these concepts will be briefly described in this chapter, and will be elaborated upon and illustrated in subsequent chapters.

1. Be Clear about Your Motives

Awareness of honest motive can be crucial to the success of our efforts. Bereavement counselors will exercise their skills most effectively when their techniques arise out of a core emotional attitude of unstinting empathy and unreserved "wanting to help."

If the counselor does not clearly "know" that he wants overridingly to help a mourner face grief, he will not be able to summon the necessary spiritual fortitude to sustain either himself or the mourner throughout the course of the sessions.

Because the counselor risks touching his most profound personal fears, because bereavement counseling is such an intimate emotional exchange, facing the question "Why do I want to involve myself in this?" is a legitimate and necessary subject for the counselor to wonder about. It should precede thinking about the purely technical elements.

Pastoral Bereavement Counseling is never a matter of technique alone. It must always integrate empathy with the technical skills. A large enough reservoir of reliable empathy, sufficient to be drawn upon throughout the vicissitudes of eight sessions, can develop *only* as a consequence of honest self-questioning about one's true motives.

This self-inquiry into one's true and deep motives is, of course, a highly personal and individual task. If you wish to become a Pastoral Bereavement Counselor, you might want to ruminate along these lines.

Granted, you may clearly feel that you want to help, but the next necessary question is, "Why? Where does this feeling come from? Why do you want to help more than other colleagues? What are your true and deep feelings about death and loss?"

There might be some practical and mundane answers that you might quickly recognize. You might be seeing this enterprise as a step to professional advancement, or as something that will look good on your record, or that will enhance your reputation. You may feel that this will increase your self-confidence and enlarge your sense of peer approval.

All of these are legitimate and worthy motives, *provided they are recognized* and faced up to. If the counselor recognizes their operative role in his decision to train for Pastoral Bereavement Counseling, they will not obstruct his effective functioning. But if you are unaware of your true and deep motives, or seek to minimize or repress your honest feelings, you may find your effectiveness as a counselor diminished.

Are you attracted to this activity because, while witnessing another's pain, you are quietly pleased that you and your family are being spared? Are you secretly harboring a dim compulsion to give advice to others, or to appear to be wise and all-knowing by playing God in a counseling situation?

Is setting yourself up as a counselor a way of quietly asserting influence or power or domination over someone, thereby increasing your sense of greater control over your own destiny? Is becoming a bereavement counselor your way of lessening your own fear of death?

"Why do I want to help mourners?" is a fundamental inquiry that all would-be bereavement counselors need to address and to "work through." It isn't essential that you arrive at a definitive once-and-for-all answer, but it is very important that you open yourself to recognize the many possible answers. Bereavement counselors should continue always to be open to future changes and different nuances in their motives.

There are deep layers of feelings within each of us, especially in connection with life and death, especially in regard to love and loss. The exercise of tapping into *our* feelings is similar and preparatory to the exercise that we will prod our bereaved clients to undertake.

We will want *them* to recognize and uncover some of *their* deep feelings. We need to experience openness to *our* feelings as we visualize asking our clients to be aware of *theirs*.

For myself, I am aware of three strands of below-surface feeling that have brought me to this work. I have alluded to two feelings in an earlier chapter—a lifelong "working through" of my childhood sorrows and an ambition to achieve some significant goal in my life. The third strand that I am presently aware of (perhaps there are others, waiting to be uncovered and tapped into) is that I dislike being a spectator toward the game of life.

I've always felt that I must do more than only think about a problem, even when it is very difficult and complex. It isn't enough to seek to understand. One must seek to do and to act, especially when confronting a seemingly impossible difficulty. I wanted to go beyond *thinking* about the pain and mystery of facing the finiteness of my years on earth.

Consciously or unconsciously, perhaps I'm seeking an activity to relieve my existential frustration. Perhaps what I'm really responding to is the silent nervousness and agitation in my heart about the basic injustice and tragedy that God seems to have foisted upon humankind, myself included.

Perhaps my life experience is teaching me that seeking to avoid a soul-wrestling about death can produce only a cheap satisfaction and an inauthentic comfort. Perhaps I'm *beginning* to understand that the only way to arrive at *some* comfortableness with death, little as it is, is through "staying with" one's fearsome but honest feelings.

If this is operating for me, an inactive mourner at this time, then perhaps I should learn that this is the best way to help the *active* mourner who is seeking authentic comfort and wholesome healing. Perhaps the lesson is that, paradoxical as it may seem, guiding the mourner through a process of feeling and facing pain is a better way to bring him to genuine peace of soul than covering his pain with a Band-Aid.

Pastoral Bereavement Counseling joins the counselor and the mourner on the same journey, but each is at a different juncture in their journeying. The counselor is wondering about death in a general way, while the mourner is wrestling with a particular loss and an actual trauma. The moment is more intense for the mourner. But the counselor, on *his* level, is fully engaged in the same subject and undergoing a similar process.

Seen in this way, the process of the counselor inquiring into his true motives is a forerunner of a similar inquiry the mourner will be led to take in searching for *his* deep feelings. The *search for bedrock feeling* is an essential part of the process—for both mourner and counselor.

In summary, asking the counselor to be clear about his motive is important for two reasons:

1. The greater the clarity in recognition of the counselor's motives, the more effective will be his treatment of the counselee; and,
2. It can serve as the mini-model for the journey into self-awareness that we hope the mourner will traverse during the counseling sessions.

2. Understand and Subscribe to the Ethos of Our Program's Overall Design and Structure

This is the second uniqueness of Pastoral Bereavement Counseling, the one that clearly differentiates it from the unstructured informal ministrations that have been used till now. The main role for the clergy has been as experts in funeral tradition and law, as leaders in prayer, and preachers of faith in time of trouble.

Anything further, such as following the mourner through his subsequent journey through grief and trauma, has been left to the personal interests and capabilities of each individual clergyperson. All that was expected of religious personnel were words of assurance and comfort, some religious philosophy, some explanation of God's actions.

This entire conception of what clergy could do for the bereaved produced random activity, vague, undirected, and unfocused. The result was, and is, that clergy have failed with effective healing to the same degree that doctors, and everyone else, have failed. The whole approach was undefined and undertaken in a spirit of hit-or-miss. In the area of supporting the bereaved, clergy have been good preachers but poor shepherds.

Pastoral Bereavement Counseling presents a model—workable, proven, theoretically and clinically valid—and suitable for the average clergyperson, as busily occupied as all of them are. When the counseling is conducted according to our suggested structure, which has built-in safeguards to prevent the buildup of the mourner's dependence upon the counselor, and is designed to minimize other attendant risks, beneficial results are often achieved.

After clarifying the matter of motive, the clergy-counselor is given a time and sequence framework through which to engage with the mourner's feelings. Pastoral Bereavement Counseling is a program that follows a step-by-step approach as it is introduced into a community on a nondenominational basis:

1. An announcement is made of the establishment of a new service for helping mourners, under whose auspices and whom to contact, depending upon local circumstances.
2. The service is presented as being available for anyone who feels the need. We recommend that the program not be aggressively promoted or advertised. It is sufficient to announce its availability.
3. The program consists of eight sessions of counseling, one-to-one, for an hour each week. Eight is the maximum; sometimes the goals are achieved sooner.
4. The program is offered as a community service, without a fee.
5. Mourners who will need further counseling will be referred to community agencies.

This structure makes it possible for the clergy in any community, in conjunction with local health and service agencies, to render more effective services to mourners than ever before. It packages a system that focuses as serious attention to grief as is being given to other psychosocial difficulties. Our program seeks to fill the existing gap in services to mourners with a worthy and effective program.

The trauma of passage through grief is as troublesome and painful as any other mental dysfunction. It temporarily—sometimes permanently—destroys the mourner's capacity to live and to love and to enjoy. It deserves as much attention from clergy and health care givers as any other life crisis. Therapy systems have been designed for alcoholism, drug abuse, rehabilitation after divorce, rehabilitation after a career change or after retirement. Why not for the bereaved?

The mourner's crisis equally needs a carefully designed therapeutic structure to ease his passage through intense pain and frightening confusion. We see Pastoral Bereavement Counseling as a therapeutic-spiritual approach that organizes a system of sustained and significant attention towards helping mourners. We hope that our model will spur communities to provide this much-needed and specialized service to a largely neglected population.

3. Intensify Your Initial Surface Empathy to Allow Your Feelings to Resonate Deeply with the Mourner's Actual Pain

Pastoral Bereavement Counseling requires more than surface empathy. Potential counselors should allow their "feeling-with" emotions to become so powerful that they will feel forced to pay serious attention to the mourner's plight. We need to move beyond the present situation where the mourner's deep feelings are treated with an attitude of "benign neglect."

We see the present disposition on the part of many clergy and many mental health practitioners to simply wish the mourner well, as a weak and insufficient response. We think that this attitude is responsible for the existing gap in effective service to mourners. We think this attitude should be improved, and we offer a program to effect this change.

We ask our counselors not only to imagine the mourner's pain but to imagine "living with" and enduring the mourner's pain—at least during the weekly sessions. We see this as a pious and highly moral action. We see this as the ultimate fulfillment of the commandment, "Love thy neighbor as thyself." We're asking our counselors to change the direction of the flow of their emotions, to "stay with," instead of to "flee from."

Again, this suggestion to the counselor to alter his emotional posture, can be seen as a preparation for the counselor's similar request of the mourner. The mourner too, as we shall see later, will be asked to endure, to "stay with" the pain, to accept its legitimacy, its validity and value.

It will be our mission to support and guide the mourner through that difficult journey. We ask the potential counselor to try it first for himself, in his own imagination. We see this act of imagination as a natural and healthy activity for *everyone* to indulge in, because death is a reality and *it is healthy and necessary to face what is true and real.*

We know that what we're asking is difficult. We understand that contemporary western culture fosters a style and spirit of hedonism—pleasure and happiness above all else. We are resisting facing death by an ostrichlike reaction at worst and by benign neglect at best. But for potential bereavement counselors, to imagine our personal reactions to death and loss is a necessary preparation to empathically recognizing the depths of our future clients' pain.

If we would but allow ourselves to let the thought creep in, "There but for the grace of God go I"! Might that not be a loud hint that there will be a time, for sure, when someone else will react the same way to *my death.*

"And therefore never send to know for whom the bell tolls; It tolls for thee."

There is no way of helping a mourner go through the passages of his grief without cultivating a genuine empathic resonance for what he is experiencing and enduring.

During an ideal Pastoral Bereavement Counseling session there will be no explanations or advice or surface platitudes or appeals to reason and logic. During an ideal session there will only be empathic presence, a sharing of pain, a sense of almost "being in the same boat," an encouragement to endure, a tinge of prayer, and a hint of hope.

After clarifying his honest motives, and after readying himself to "feel with" another's deep pain, a growing Pastoral Bereavement Counselor will be in a position to appreciate a mourner's basic emotions, and to note some dynamic characteristics of those feelings. He may then be able to evaluate the appropriateness of the special skills that our program recommends, and that constitute the central element of its uniqueness.

The clinical material in this and the subsequent chapters is derived from the case histories of over 500 mourners who have been counseled over the past six years through our Pastoral Bereavement Counseling services in the New York area.

THE MOURNER'S FEELINGS

No two mourners have reported exactly the same feelings, nor in exactly the same sequence. But while the proportions of the expressed emotions differ, as do the timing of their sequences, our experience points to clear patterns that can be recognized as endemic to the bereavement process.

As mourners begin to come out of the initial reaction of shock and denial, they move into feelings of sadness, hopelessness and helplessness, fears for the future, emptiness, anxiety, wishful thinking, lethargy, experiencing illusory images and inability to concentrate. They may report episodes of weeping, irritation, daydreaming, or some changes in sleeping or eating patterns.

All mourners go through feelings of anger, being cheated—"I didn't deserve this, my beloved didn't deserve this"—and anger turned against oneself—"I must have done something wrong to cause his death"—which is a feeling of guilt. Indeed, the feelings of anger and guilt are so usual and prevalent among mourners that there is a demonstrable basis for formulating a general rule: *Anger and guilt are core emotions that every mourner needs to recognize and must "work through" before he will reach healing and restoration.*

The Nature and Characteristics of the Mourner's Feelings

At times, the mourner feels himself in a maelstrom of emotion, overwhelmed by powerful urges—despair, sadness, rage. Guilt is sometimes so powerful that, consciously or unconsciously, mourners look forward to some punishment as an expiation of their feeling of having "sinned." (*This is one of the reasons that some mourners will not avail themselves of the opportunity given to them to be helped by counseling.*) The dynamic sources of guilt, and why it is *always* experienced by the mourner, will be discussed in a later chapter.

There are some periods when the emotions of grief are the bereaved's constant companion. They stay with the mourner at all times—eating, sleeping, working, relaxing. There seems to be no moment of surcease. The bereaved become so obsessed with grief that they cannot function normally.

Often, the tension is compounded by the confusion and ambivalence within each feeling. The mourner dimly perceives opposite feelings seizing hold of him at the same time. She may be angry at losing her beloved, yet relieved that he is no longer in pain. He may be sad that she can no longer enjoy life's pleasures, but grateful that he himself has survived.

Mourners may feel empty, yet fantasize a new freedom and novel adventures. In thinking of the dead, they may also recall fragments of a love-hate relationship with the beloved. They are caught in a conflict of wanting to remember, yet needing to forget and let go. They rage at the fates, yet suppress their anger out of fear of making God angrier.

There is no pure, single, unadulterated emotion in the human mourner. The very nature of the situation mixes fear and hope in irreconcilable opposition. The mourner is enduring a double distress—the hurt of the loss, and the pain of being mystified by an irrational ambivalence. It hurts when he confronts the loss, it's scary when he can make no sense of it. His pains are illogical, compulsive and obsessive, ambivalent and frightening.

Add to all this the lonely realization that he's in an unprecedented situation in his life. These are new experiences for most mourners, and some begin to fear that they may be losing their minds. Who can they speak to about their feelings? Who can they trust? Who will listen without thinking them crazy? Who will just listen?

Many contemporary mourners hear no response to these questions. Their experience in today's culture and society convinces them that modern society is indifferent and uncaring. They experience this unanswered cry for help as a rejection, as a deep frustration, as a compounding of their original bereavement.

This is why so many mourners suffer in silence, suppressing their rage and frustration. The inevitable result is a deepening of the mourner's depression, a momentum towards further emotional difficulty, a feeding of panic upon itself.

Yes, some bereaved persons instinctively hold on, make their individual adjustments, and in time and with God's help, return to normal and healthy living. But even for them, the pain usually has to be endured for many months. It is the hope and goal of Pastoral Bereavement Counselors to shorten the time of trauma and hasten the time of healing.

The impetus to undertake the practice of Pastoral Bereavement Counseling derives from a dawning realization that effective healing of a mourner's wounds requires using different skills than have been generally employed up to now. It entails opening ourselves up to accepting a need for supplementary training.

4. Understand the Dynamics of the Recommended Counseling Skills, and Seek to Apply Them Competently and Consistently

We recommend that clergy consider adopting a radically different approach in dealing with mourners in the post-funeral period. We believe they will find it necessary to unlearn old approaches and to practice new techniques.

Mental health practitioners may find that, while the recommended counseling skills are not unknown to them, the selection and strict economy in using them, and the tight design and structure of Pastoral Bereavement Counseling make it a system unto itself. Although the techniques are not new, the package as presented to the community is a pioneer concept.

A decision to become a Pastoral Bereavement Counselor must include a willingness to undergo training, both didactic and experiential, and a commitment to accept supervision for the initial hands-on practice. Because it is a *different* approach to helping mourners, it cannot be entered into without a clear sense of commitment and responsibility.

In our structured sessions we do not answer questions directly. We do not preach or offer advice. We have fashioned a new approach. We invite the mourner to participate in a step-by-step program.

1. We provide a safe and supportive atmosphere in which the mourner will feel free to express his deep emotions without fear of being judged or evaluated.
2. We convey our impression (in most cases) that what they're going through is essentially normal. We understand and empathize with their pain but transmit our conviction (in most cases) that there is reason to hope that it will get better.
3. We help the mourner to look squarely and honestly at his feelings. We will help him to identify, clarify, and differentiate the jumble of emotions that are frightening him. We will suggest that his conflicting emotions are probably also normal, and *will dissipate, if not suppressed.*
4. We reach out to the mourner with an implied promise: "We'll support you as you go through and endure this crisis in your life. We will feel your pain with you during these eight sessions because we love you as a child of God. We will help you to "stay with" your feelings by "staying with" these feelings *with you.* We will not abandon you for these eight sessions. You've reached out for help and we want to grasp your hand and hope to help you. (We believe that God wants to help you too.)"

These four steps form the relational frame within which the therapeutic exchange develops and proceeds to target its objectives. This is the counselor's orientation as he approaches and works with the mourner. He does not necessarily speak these words, but they are the signposts on the road to his specific goal.

The details of these counseling skills will be more fully discussed in Chapter 7. They are also given exhaustive attention in the training courses conducted by our commission. But it would be useful at this point to provide an illustration of the specific newness of our approach.

THE IMPORTANCE OF NON-DIRECTIVE COUNSELING SKILLS

Learning the techniques that we recommend for bereavement counseling may be a challenge to clergy because it involves a change from their usual manner of relating to people. Traditionally, most clergy have seen themselves as possessors of truth and wisdom. When people turn to them with questions they have naturally and automatically responded with answers and direction.

But the bereaved person is in a special and unique situation. His voicing of painful questions is really a plea for a companion-in-feeling more than for a dispenser of logic and wisdom. As has been described, he is so buffeted by powerful passions, by currents and crosscurrents, by bewildering compulsions, that his primary need is to express and confront his emotions in the presence of someone *who feels with him,* who understands and legitimizes, who *blesses his emotional struggle.*

In order for the Pastoral Bereavement Counselor to genuinely serve as the bereaved's partner-in-pain, he must listen more than teach, he must acknowledge his partner's hurt, instead of trying to philosophize it away.

A case in point would be how a bereavement counselor should relate to a mourner in the opening sessions. At that moment, the ability to discern the feeling beneath the mourner's spoken words can be crucial. A counselor who responds to the surface words and not to the underlying emotions invites the mourner's suspicion that this counselor is like everyone else, unwilling or incapable of empathy. Only a non-directive approach can signal a capacity or an ambition to feel with another.

The non-directive approach would allow the bereaved to take the initiative in fully expressing his pain and perplexity, and to let the flow continue. It neither induces nor hinders the flow of feeling. It respects the client's feeling at all times, *whatever* they are, *as* they are.

The bereavement counselor who is non-directive tries not to judge or rate the mourner's feelings on any scale that suggests success or failure, good or bad. He tries to establish deep rapport. He tries to transmit the feeling that he's genuinely interested in listening to the mourner's pain, and waits.

In most instances it won't take long till he hears the hurt feelings bursting forth; but he should in no way "telegraph" to the client what he expects him to say. Non-directive therapy is most helpful when we allow the client to reveal his emotions in response to his own felt needs, and at his own rhythm and pace.

5. Increase the Efficacy of Your Empathy and Counseling Skills by Consciously Connecting Them to a Specific and Attainable Goal, and by Never Losing Sight of That Connection

A central element in Pastoral Bereavement Counseling is the mutual focusing on a definite goal that is recognized by both counselor and mourner—more clearly by the former than the latter. Structure and empathy are necessary for our program; but by themselves they will not achieve optimum results.

The application and utilization of all the elements in Pastoral Bereavement Counseling need to be directed and dedicated to a specific goal that both mourner and counselor can accept. Only then will the intellectual and emotional energies of both parties be galvanized to produce a powerful healing mechanism.

Pastoral Bereavement Counseling is anything but random or diffuse. All the wise therapeutic technique, all the counseling choices, all the suffering and confrontation with pain that the mourner is encouraged to endure, must be channelled to a worthy purpose perceived as attainable. It will be ineffective and largely wasted if it is pointed only towards a general aim such as the traditional intention of helping, or supporting, or "comforting" the mourner.

Our program's purpose is clear and specific. We set up a target for both participants to see and recognize, and toward which they will feel it worthwhile to dedicate their whole being. That purpose is *to move the griever through all, or some, of the feelings that inevitably arise out of their loss experience*—to facilitate their movement through the journey, to help them to identify, to deeply experience, and to "stay with" their feelings, during the time period of their counseling.

Our goal is not philosophy. Our purpose is to create a therapeutic frame within which the mourner will be able to experience *with us* what the mourner would *have* to experience *with* or *without* us. Accomplishing this goal will make it possible for God (or nature, or whatever you wish to name it) to complete the healing in a quicker and more wholesome way than otherwise.

Harnessing the counselor's reservoir of empathy to a worthy and visible goal is what distinguishes our program from the well-intentioned but frighteningly useless ministrations that clergy have been traditionally providing. Even those clergy who have sought to connect their natural unschooled empathy to *some* demonstration of support for the mourner, have seen their efforts frittered away to almost zero.

In the absence of effective results, their own sense of failure and frustration may have soured them on further efforts to service the bereaved. Generalized empathy without a clear goal has thus failed both the grievers and their potential helpers.

Pastoral Bereavement Counselors can alter this situation. Because we openly target a goal for both mourner and counselor, because our methods are specifically designed to move toward that goal every step of the way, because there are built-in means to monitor progress or lack of it, we can reach greater fulfillment and experience less frustration.

6. Understand That Goal-Directed Empathy Requires Patience, Tolerance, Acceptance, and Love

While we will discuss each of these desirable attributes in detail in later chapters, they deserve to be mentioned in general at this point. These relational attitudes are centrally important for potential bereavement counselors to develop within themselves.

A. *Patience.* We have already pointed out that in bereavement counseling it is useful to convey an understanding that mourning is a process that is neither quick nor simple. Mourners should not be led to expect that there is an easy answer to pain or a short journey to healing.

This is something the counselor needs to learn as well, especially as it applies to his possibly romantic expectations of quick success. A realistic attitude of patience is part of the basic equipment that the counselor must bring to his task.

The counselor develops patience from his basic feeling of empathy. His empathy can lead him to feel an emotional stubbornness—a dedication, if you will—that will not be easily deflected from his purpose of helping the mourner. The quality of patience also derives from an intellectual understanding of the nature of the two processes that operate in bereavement counseling: the dynamics of counseling and the dynamics of adjusting to grief.

Briefly stated, the mourner is recovering from shock, thawing out from numbness, looking at a world that is fundamentally different from when his beloved was alive. These thoughts and feelings are difficult to integrate into his sense of present and future. The mourner needs to allow time to pass for the natural unfolding of these phases. They cannot be hurried through.

Similarly for the counselor: His required activities—listening, reflecting, feeling and "staying with"—are not mechanical or momentary actions. They are neither instant nor instinctive. Rather, they are the products of earnest consideration.

They involve reflection, intellectual discernment, emotional integration, and spiritual endurance. By their very nature they require more than fleeting attention; they cannot be hurried through. Each mourner is different, and counseling responses need to be weighed and tailored to the individual's particular situation.

The counselor's intervention within the therapeutic setting, when he wishes to provide some guidance for the mourner, is never put forth quickly, starkly, directly. This may be particularly troublesome for clergy, who are accustomed to direct preaching and authoritative advice-giving. In a counseling situation, where the preacher seeks to be shepherd to his flock, it is better to offer little advice. It is best to project empathic patience and enduring support.

A pastoral counselor should train himself so that his words and attitude will not seek to convince or overpower. It is more helpful to suggest, to tentatively advance a notion, to plant a seed, to reiterate, to repeat feelings and implications. This too cannot be hurried. All these processes presuppose an attitude of basic patience.

As the Pastoral Bereavement Counselor gains experience, his feelings of basic patience will probably grow and intensify. He will have noted how a suggestion that he may have implanted at a previous session and which the client may have ignored or rejected, has now been accepted and begun to be integrated.

Often, as the sessions progress, the mourner reports changes in behavior and living patterns; but they have occurred so gradually that the mourner is unaware of his own progress. Counselors need unadulterated patience to prod and nurture this gradual step-by-step movement towards healing.

In addition to considerations revolving about technique, patience is also basic to the working out of the dynamic processes. In bereavement counseling, a conscious effort to "stay with," an explicit assertion of will to endure some measure of pain is crucial to the therapy. An attitude of impatience on the part of either the counselor or mourner will hinder the healing.

B. Tolerance.   As the counselor increases his ability to be patient, he will find himself less critical of a mourner's revelations. It is hoped that he will feel less contempt or anger or judgment at mistakes the client admits, or at confronting a lifestyle different from his own.

Sometimes a beginning counselor meeting such a situation will recognize negative judgments welling up within his feelings towards the client. He might try to make an intellectual effort to suppress or disguise them, knowing that acting out his bias would endanger the success of the therapy. But this is not a good practice for the long run, for which the counselor needs to develop, in his heart as well as through his brain, a near-automatic attitude of tolerance.

The ideal degree of tolerance is reached when the counselor instinctively and wholeheartedly relates to the client as he finds him, whatever his condition or shortcomings, whatever his life-style or life philosophy, without wanting to change him. The counselor will function best when he honestly regards the mourner as a worthy human being in his own right, as he is, entitled to as much healing and happiness *as the counselor himself.*

Counselors can reach this optimum level of tolerance as a result of pondering their true motives, recognizing the strengths and weaknesses of their empathy for bereaved persons, and imagining some counseling situations where their patience or tolerance may be tested. Counselors continue this process of examining their own attitudes during the supervision process they are asked to accept for their initial cases.

C. Acceptance.   Acceptance—a genuine attitude of no criticism and no judgment of the client—is critical for our program. During a time of grief, when mourners are so deeply assaulted by their hopelessness and confusion, their self-doubt and self-flagellation, they are especially vulnerable to a further assault on their self-esteem. If they feel themselves being judged, or imperfectly accepted, or placed on the defensive by any criticism—spoken or conveyed by attitude—from the one they've turned to for help, the process can be crippled at its very inception.

Pastoral Bereavement Counselors need to become sensitive to the effects of their words and attitudes on their mourning clients. This is an area in which professional clergy may have special need of retraining, because it is the very opposite of their usual activity of preachment and faultfinding in the name of a higher authority.

Despite this potential difficulty, clergy can become the principal reservoir from which we hope to attract and recruit Pastoral Bereavement Counselors. We believe we will be able to demonstrate to ministers of religion, whose feelings of love for their fellowman were clearly a significant determinant in their choice of vocation, how to increase the effectiveness of their empathy and love through using a structured system. We hope this will encourage them to undertake training and to participate in our movement.

D. Love. In the context of bereavement counseling I mean this word to denote the ideal web of emotions, intense relationship, and commitment that the counselor may come to feel toward his mourner-client. Love develops from the "chemistry" of the three-way interaction between mourner, counselor, and the purpose of their mission, that can produce a feeling of extra dedication and additional warmth.

It is an individual's affirmation of intention—in this case, that of a potential or actual bereavement counselor—to strive for the highest perfection in the performance of his task, to acknowledge and to eagerly accept the necessity for personal sacrifice in the performance of his task, and to pray or otherwise hope for a revelation that will confirm its significance.

The love of the counselor towards the mourner-client goes beyond clarity of motive, striving for competence in the necessary skills, connecting empathy with a worthy goal, and dedication to patience, tolerance, and acceptance. There is a further ingredient—a sense of growth towards a greater personal fulfillment and towards the pleasing of God on a higher plane than ever before.

There can arise the intimation that by this activity, undertaken freely in the service of another-in-need, the counselor has become an instrument through which will be achieved a purpose higher than his dearest wish. Love can come from the realization that counselor and mourner are co-instruments playing together in God's orchestra.

The love that a bereavement counselor can experience towards a mourner-client is the touching of a mystery and a glimpse into the wonders of that mystery. Pastoral Bereavement Counseling can become for the counselor an extraordinary vehicle to climb the next rung in the ladder that ascends toward heaven in each of our lives.

7. *Look Forward to the Possibility of Bereavement Counseling Becoming—at Certain Times and under Certain Circumstances—a Deep Religious Experience for Both the Mourner and the Counselor*

There have been moments during counseling sessions when both the mourner and I have sensed an invisible hand of guidance. There was a touch of mystery, if not a miracle. There was a sense of exaltation and an awareness that true healing was in the making.

The intensity of empathy and emotional intimacy created a feeling that an additional partner was joining our circle of sharing and experiencing. We sensed that the life transaction we were processing might have wider repercussions than we could imagine.

There was an awareness of the significance and precious-ness of the moment. There was a sense of fulfillment beyond our wildest expectations. We recognized that those feelings of peace and wholesomeness were a sign of God's goodness.

I believe that Pastoral Bereavement Counseling has such possibilities for all its practitioners and participants. It can be reached by many people who earnestly follow our suggestions.

When Pastoral Bereavement Counseling is successful, the mourner feels the counselor's empathy at all times, the coun-selor draws many times on his inner empathy, and both will feel God's empathy some of the time. This three-dimensional em-pathic presence cannot be planned for, or manipulated, or con-sciously induced. It arises from the entire web of emotional transactions that take place during therapy. It appears when all the diverse elements begin to mesh.

When the motives that originally inspired the counselor in-cluded a fair measure of empathy, when the discipline imposed by the structure and the techniques are accepted as a worth-while sacrifice, and when the mourner begins to respond to the therapeutic process, an empathic glow enters into the happen-ings and suffuses the entire ambience. Often, this creates an additional momentum that fosters the healing process even more.

THE FLOW OF EMPATHY

The mourner feels the counselor's empathy many times during the counseling process:

> . . . when he experiences the counselor's unconditional ac-ceptance of whatever emotions he is expressing;

... when he witnesses the counselor's utmost concentration and relentless effort to listen, to "hear" his pain as long as necessary;

... when he perceives the counselor's restraint in not offering pat answers or simple solutions;

... when he notices that the counselor eagerly permits, even encourages, his unhindered ventilation of his deepest turmoil;

... when he recognizes that the counselor is sacrificing time, energy, and peace of mind to minister to him with a whole heart;

... when he witnesses the counselor's sharing his pain and discomfort. On those occasions when the counselor is moved to words or gestures of "feeling with" and displays them sincerely and unashamedly, the mourner will feel the empathy;

... when the counselor is moved to tears (for the mourner's plight, not his own), the mourner will experience another's genuine concern and warmth;

... when the counselor uses every opportunity to convey his genuine concern and to demonstrate unlimited love to a fellow moral wrestling with pain no mortal can escape, the mourner will feel an empathic presence. He will have gained a partner-in-feeling, he will have found a friend-in-emotion.

They both know it is for a brief moment, for that hour, and for only a few sessions. But, as limited as it is, for that hour it is real and embracing, for that moment it is intense and unrestricted.

The Flow of Empathy within the Counselor

The counselor uses his own empathy as a source of self-discipline and self-encouragement. It is the wellspring of the compassion which enables him to absorb some of the mourner's pain. It stimulates him to integrate the mourner's feelings into his own. It can inspire him to do more than "listen," to go beyond "hearing." It encourages him to allow the mourner's sadness to touch and affect him.

The counselor's awareness of his empathy operates as an instinctive response to the stark realization that the mourner is crying out for help. Empathy helps him recognize that there's no one else motivated or capable of extending help who is accessible and available.

If the counselor flees this opportunity the mourner will continue to flounder or will sink further. His empathy makes him realize that he has no alternative to becoming involved. Even without knowing exactly what to do, the counselor's empathy motivates him to remain and struggle, it doesn't allow him to look the other way.

I remember this as the operative emotion that forced me to "struggle through" my early bereavement counseling situations, when I had little experience and less confidence. I wasn't sure of what to do, but I was certain that I had to try.

The flow of empathy operates throughout the entire course of counseling. It can fuel the intellectual and emotional discipline that may be required when difficulties arise. It helps the counselor to forgive himself when he moves too fast or too slowly. Genuine empathy gives courage and legitimization that can sustain the counselor's morale even in the midst of an occasional lapse.

If we feel the other's pain deeply enough—irrespective of failure or success in a particular instance—we will have emotional justification for undertaking to try again. A bereavement counselor who doesn't feel sufficient empathy, who gives up quickly, may want to reconsider his decision to become one. This is one of the issues that can arise in the supervisory process.

Our procedures in the internship program for beginning Pastoral Bereavement Counselors provide for consultation with clinical supervisors on a regular basis. Supervision is not an examination, it is an exercise in learning and growth. Errors or imperfections in applying counseling skills should be regarded as learning opportunities rather than irredeemable failures.

Through the supervision process, interns will come to recognize that the intensity or the absence of empathic presence is a central factor in a counselor's ultimate effectiveness.

At Times We Can Imagine That We Are Feeling God's Empathy

The sense of blessing that can envelop the mourner *and* the counselor during bereavement counseling is a precious experience, because both can feel a spiritual presence. At such times, the counseling experience becomes something akin to prayer and exaltation.

It arises in the mourner as an answer to his prayer for healing. It arises in the counselor as he feels himself becoming an instrument of God's purposes.

There can be no greater fulfillment for a rabbi, priest, or minister—or for anyone, for that matter—than to serve as the channel for God's mercy, *and to be blessedly aware of it.*

There can be no surer sign of a miracle from heaven than for a mourner in distress to be partially healed in a few weeks' time.

These feelings, the sensing of God's empathic presence within a therapeutic situation, are attainable when we engage in Pastoral Bereavement Counseling.

When two persons have freely contracted, in the sight of God, to grapple earnestly with deep feelings, to confront the reality He has imposed upon us, to share the distressful journey with hope and prayer and high motives, and *know* that they are truly wrestling, they will also be aware of the coming of His blessing.

When the mourner struggles alone he perceives no meaning in it, only sadness. When the mourner struggles *together with another*, there is a perceived sharing of the pain, there is a pointing toward some sense, there is a raising of a ray of hope.

When the hope becomes more tangible, when some progress is made, the attendant emotion is more than relief, more than gratitude. It offers to the griever a glimpse of some residual "rightness" in the scheme of things, it makes partial sense of the mysteries of existence and of love and of life. It can develop into a conquest of the fear of death, because we begin to understand that while loss is devastating, it need not utterly destroy.

It can become the feeling that in the end, after going through the grief—God does love us. We have our duties, we have our roles to play, we must suffer pain and endure the wrestling, but in the end—God does love us.

This is more than "comfort and consolation." This can be a renewal of faith and a fresh blossoming in the garden of God's nurturing empathy.

This can hardly be reached through preachment or by dispensing platitudes. Such a summit of spiritual experience is only attainable through purposeful counseling that is earnest, thoughtful, and well-designed.

We have seen that Pastoral Bereavement Counseling benefits both mourner and counselor by their simultaneous awareness of God's empathic presence. One—the mourner—gains emotional nourishment and experiences an impetus towards immediate healing. The other—the counselor—receives lifelong spiritual sustenance as he appreciates God's nonabandonment of man, even in the face of sadness and pain.

THIS THERAPY IS SACRED

All therapy may be viewed as potentially holy—important to God—because it aims to remove obstacles that prevent man, a creation of God, and His partner, from reaching his highest potential. When therapeutic counseling frees man from his emotional shackles it enables him to better serve God "with all his heart and with all his soul."

But bereavement counseling enters into a higher category of sacredness because it focuses upon the most challenging questions of the God-man relationship—man's terror of death, man's challenge to God's justice, and man's courage to overcome and to survive.

We cannot really *live* until we are less fearful of death. If we could ease the terror, we would have peace of mind sooner, the quicker to return to the creative business of life. We can serve neither God nor man with peak efficiency if we do not alleviate the crippling dysfunctions of mourning and grieving.

Modern mourners seem not to be finding in the traditional rituals and ceremonies of adjustment as effective a mechanism for solace as did previous generations. Perhaps it is because we have lost "faith," perhaps it is due to the shifts in societal and cultural milieus. Whatever the reason, if we could develop a better way to shorten the trauma of grief for contemporary mourners, we would be lengthening the days in which modern man could be serving God with full heart.

When it takes years for a mourner to be consoled, or if healing never comes at all, those years and that life are *lost both to man and God*. Pastoral Bereavement Counseling is sacred because its goal is to more quickly restore the mourner to the business of living, which is also God's purpose for man.

Counseling the mourner should be regarded as more than a medical or psychiatric task. It is a sacred mission because it is simultaneously beneficial to man and significant to God. If we believe that human life is sacred—the essence of all religions— then it must follow that the process of returning a mourner to full capacity for living partakes of that sacredness.

The rabbis of the Talmud had a favorite saying: "He who saves one life is as though he had saved a whole world." Who can measure the importance of even one life, with all its influences and interactions, with all its instances of affecting, and being affected by, all the others? Is any one switch in a master computer less important than any other?

In the same vein, perhaps our movement can subscribe to a paraphrase: "He who saves even one day of a mourner's grief is as though he had saved his whole life." Who can measure the importance of one day? Has anyone the right to refuse to heal as quickly as possible?

SUMMATION

It might be useful to think of the six-months-to-a-year period after the funeral as the time frame during which a natural process of adjustment usually takes place. God gives the mourner some natural medicine for grief—the passage of time, the individual's innate ego strength, the ability to hope for a better future—that takes the mourner through this time period in one fashion or another.

The problem is that it takes time, that there is much suffering, that complications can arise to inhibit a full recovery.

Pastoral Bereavement Counselors hope to shorten the period of pain, lessen the suffering, and find a way around the complications.

We aim to speed up the mourner's walk through his valley of sadness *by walking with him* in the ways that we have outlined. We will further discuss these ways and include illustrations from case histories in the next chapters.

Our ambition is to be God's partners in a non-profit enterprise, but one that is healthful and sacred for all who are involved.

If God is the Physician and He dispenses the medicine—the natural adjustment process—then the Pastoral Bereavement Counselor is the Physician's aide. It is the counselor's job to encourage the patient to take his medicine on time, to fine-tune the dosage, and to monitor the progress or lack of it. The Physician needs us and can use our help. He hopes we'll do a creditable job and that He'll be able to be proud of us.

Chapter 4

THE STRUCTURE

In the program to help mourners that I am asking colleagues to adopt, the specially designed structure is an essential component. In this chapter, I will explain the rationale for the unique design, and how the structure operates to facilitate healing.

We believe that our present design, which has emerged after twelve years of trial and error, is the one most suitable and efficient to meet the needs of the mourner and to fit the capabilities of most clergy and mental health providers.

Some of the topics we will discuss in this chapter are:

> ... What are the dynamics of structured counseling that make it so effective?
> ... Why are the sessions limited to "no more than eight"?
> ... What is the counselor's goal as he sets about his task?
> ... The structure of the program as it is presented to the community?
> ... How to respond to requests for additional counseling;
> ... How the structured design aids the counselor to identify mourners who need further professional attention.

The Dynamics of Structural Counseling

The three *dynamic processes* that operate in a structured situation usually emerge in the following sequence: the mourner and counselor enter into an implied *contract* for a temporary but intense relationship, during which both will *concentrate* their mental and emotional faculties towards the *purpose* of reaching a definite and definable goal.

The structure is designed to integrate these processes into a framework that will facilitate the application of appropriate techniques which will bring healing to the mourner.

The Contract

What is meant here is the formation of a mutual attitude, a moral and ethical bond—not a legal agreement. The term is intended to describe the beginning of a therapeutic relationship as a consensus emerges for offering and accepting "treatment."

It represents the early stages of developing a free and uncoerced bond between counselor and counselee. The contract is a framework within which the initial interests of both parties can be noted, and which facilitates a therapeutic intensification of a budding counseling relationship if it is warranted.

The terms of the contract are not immediately or explicitly stated. The mourner comes to understand them through the phases of his introduction to the therapy:

1. He has heard about the availability of this service through the written or the spoken word, or through a friend's recommendation;
2. He had decided to call for further information, and/or to ask for an appointment;
3. There was a response, via a five- or ten-minute phone conversation which concluded with the setting of the first appointment;
4. He is now with the counselor at the first session.

At some point during that first hour, usually not at the opening of the session, the contract is gently offered in words to this effect: "I'm glad you've come. As you can see, what we do here at this program is to encourage you to talk about your feelings, your distress, or sadness, or anything you wish to bring up. We'll try to help as much as we can. The program asks that you agree to come for one hour each week, up to eight times. There is no charge for these sessions, they are offered as a community service. Our program does not go beyond eight sessions."

"How does it help? What good is it going to do?"

"We've found that it helps some people. We'd like to try it with you and see how it goes."

Or:

"It might work because it helps people to get in touch with their feelings honestly. But of course we both have to work at it. There's no magic, but the program has had some success."

"Why do you say up to eight sessions?"

"Well, sometimes people feel that they've progressed enough after a few sessions—five or six. Then, if we both agree, we won't have to have further sessions.

"Incidentally, that's an important point to mention. If at any time you don't want to continue meeting to talk, I want you to first discuss it with me, not to cancel out on the phone. That's part of the understanding we want you to have about this program."

"What happens if I need more than eight?"

"This program is limited to eight sessions. If we both think you need more, we'll refer you to someone else for further counseling."

Although this sense of mutual agreement is developed gradually and may never be fully or precisely articulated, the counselor must learn to recognize its presence or absence. He cannot effectively proceed to the subsequent steps in the therapy unless it is clear that the mourner understands and accepts these parameters. The "contract," the agreement—the basic rules of procedure—are the indispensable foundation for the counseling activity that will follow.

The training course that the commission is prepared to

conduct provides full instruction in the art of bringing the mourner to joining in this contract.

The Concentration

Structuring the sessions as we do, a 1-hour meeting each week for up to 8 weeks, is a very efficient device that forces both mourner and counselor to concentrate their attention towards the problem at hand.

The problem for the mourner is that he is feeling pain— he is enduring sadness, emotional discomfort, distress. He would like to be relieved of this pain.

Contrary to what we might expect logically, it is very difficult for the mourner to concentrate and deal frontally with his powerful feelings. Without a structure that directs and channels his attention to his pain, many mourners let things slide and postpone facing reality. They take the easy way out, and *hope* that they'll start feeling better. Unfortunately, by doing so they are probably increasing the time needed to move through their trauma.

A structure of weekly sessions—one hour this week to concentrate on his feelings, and a second hour next week to concentrate on his feelings, and the prospect of 6 more hours of facing, not avoiding, his feelings—pushes the mourner to force himself to concentrate. This push can never be felt or induced through informal, unstructured, at-random meetings with clergy or with anyone else. Without a structure, even the mourners tend to postpone facing their trauma.

The problem for the counselor is less personally emotional, but more cerebral and more a matter of will. Without a structure, without a vehicle to translate empathy into action, all the goodwill in the world can be frittered away. When there is no definite time period set aside for facing the mourner, the easiest thing to do is to procrastinate and assign a low priority to caring for the mourner. Knowing that it's uncomfortable to share in another's sadness, it is simpler to rationalize that there are more important things to do. "I'll help the widow next week."

There is understandable and legitimate hesitation to enter into an open-ended process. Without a structure there is no mechanism to force a would-be counselor *to pay attention* to the mourner's needs.

With a structure, even one that is artificial, there is less excuse to delay and more hope for a successful outcome. When the counselor knows that what he is being asked to undertake has an order and a sequence, that he need aim only for a limited goal, and that there are tried-and-true methods that have succeeded, he may hesitate less. The task is arduous; but it is one that has a beginning and an end; it is one that he may hope to complete.

For both the counselor and the mourner, the structure of Pastoral Bereavement Counseling makes the prospect of concentrating on painful feelings a little more palatable. The structure is the framework which facilitates the initial decision to begin to concentrate. It is the same framework that can maintain the determination to continue concentrating on difficult feelings throughout the eight sessions.

Concentrating for a Purpose

This is the third dynamic which is activated by structure that is integral to Pastoral Bereavement Counseling. We will formulate the goal of the effort later in this chapter. At this point, all we wish to indicate is that the structure is designed to vigorously spur both mourner and counselor to hasten towards the goal, to achieve the purpose. Using a structure minimizes the danger of straying away from the target, of giving in to inertia and following a path of least resistance.

Both mourner and counselor may tend to drift away from a frontal confrontation with the trauma of loss, the former because it is distressing, the latter because it is exhausting. Without a structure, it would be extremely difficult to achieve results; with structure, it becomes possible. If either party to the contract drifts away from the purpose, the structure can be invaluable in bringing them back to concentrating on and fulfilling the goal.

WHY ARE THE SESSIONS LIMITED?

We've already mentioned two peripheral reasons—to aid in forcing concentration, and to maintain the sense of purpose and movement towards target. But there are two other reasons that are more important, and to which attention must be drawn.

One, the limited number of sessions mitigate against the buildup of an excessive dependence on the part of the mourner towards the counselor.

Two, the limited number of sessions can lessen the power of a countertransference the counselor may feel towards the mourner or towards bereavement in general.

Client-dependence and counselor-countertransference are dangers that are inherent in any counseling situation, and all counselors need to develop an awareness of their potential emergence.

But in Pastoral Bereavement Counseling—in a relationship that is comprised of sharing of deep feelings, expectations of help and guidance from another, and intense grappling with the fearsome reality of death—these feelings may be expected to be even more prominent.

In fact, in Pastoral Bereavement Counseling, these kinds of feelings may be naturally and legitimately anticipated. Dependence and countertransference arise from the nature of the tasks connected with bereavement and the means employed by mourners and counselors to accomplish those tasks.

The mourner's dependence arises from the fact that he is a mourner. He is in a unique predicament, with few around him genuinely willing to help, and almost no one knowing how. It is natural for him to perceive the counselor, whether clergy or not, as a savior—especially when no payment is expected. The mourner is noticing that the Pastoral Bereavement Counselor—whether clergy or layperson—is donating his time and energy as an act of lovingkindness toward another.

If the counseling begins to succeed, the mourner's feelings easily glide from gratitude, into looking forward to the next session, into a mild dependence. If the therapy seems to be failing, the mourner may more desperately "clutch at a straw" and begin to unconsciously fear the losing of this one hope. In either scenario, the mourner begins to perceive the counselor in unrealistic terms. He begins to fantasize, or expect, or hope for a longer relationship.

This is client dependence on the counselor—uncontrollable, unconscious, yet natural and understandable. The nature of a bereavement counseling situation—especially as it exposes and shares intimate fears and yearnings—lends itself to an unconscious progression of such feelings of dependence.

On the other hand, the counselor is not contemplating an extended emotional commitment. He instinctively recognizes—despite his humanitarian motive and readiness for altruistic sacrifice—that his healthiest option is for a limited engagement.

The community also has a stake in this. The Pastoral Bereavement Counselor's value to the community will be diminished if the limits on his commitment of time and energy will be compromised. What is needed is an element in the basic design that will protect a volunteer counselor from being swept along by the dynamics of a counseling situation into waters beyond his depth.

Excessive client dependence complicates the counseling situation to the extent that normal procedures for concluding the therapy may become insufficient. Great skills may be required for the counselor to extricate himself from the relationship without damaging the counselee. Our movement cannot expect such herculean efforts from volunteers.

The problem in the case of bereavement is even sharper because a troubled mourner, already reeling from the trauma of one loss, is highly vulnerable to additional pain if he feels himself cut off from yet another significant figure. When the mourner comes to feel a deepening attachment to the new figure in his life who is about to "save" him, any brusque withdrawal —no matter how reasonable or necessary in the counselor's view —can cast him deeper into helplessness and hopelessness.

Without careful thought about this potential opposition between a mourner's need for emotional attachment and the impracticality of a volunteer counselor entering into a long-term relationship, our movement would have little chance to succeed. We believe we have found an effective solution for this dilemma through our design of an eight-session limit.

This makes possible a balance: it meets the mourner's need to share in a deep relationship, yet clarifies the limits and the length of the relationship at its very inception. It gives the counseling process a chance to unfold and to take hold, but builds-in a time-and-sequence frame that will lessen the chances of a mounting mourner dependency. At the same time, this same device protects the counselor against a buildup of uncontrollable feelings within himself.

Counselor's Countertransference

Here too, there is a unique dimension in bereavement counseling that extends beyond the countertransference that is ordinarily encountered. The usual phenomenon of countertransference can be recognized when the counselor's attention to the client or to the material the client is presenting becomes affected with distinct emotional overtones. The counselor begins to have thoughts and feelings that are less concerned with the client's needs, and becoming more centered on emotions and feelings that are welling up within himself. What is usually happening when this occurs is that the counseling dynamics have triggered memories or associations from within the counselor's past.

Sometimes, the consciousness of these memories and associations becomes sufficiently intense within the counselor's feelings as to complicate the course of the therapy. When countertransference is operating, the counselor begins to use the situation to minister to his own inner needs and less to the client's. Countertransference feelings can become so overwhelming that they may disrupt the therapeutic strategy.

Because *everyone* has fears of death and loss, and because both counselor and counselee are necessarily immersed in these feelings, the counselor needs to be assured that, whatever his discomfort, it will not endure forever. Without such an assurance, the developing intensity of these feelings might overwhelm the counselor and disrupt his efforts to prevent the mourner from being overwhelmed.

In a sense, this is precisely the fine line that the bereavement counselor needs carefully to tread. He leads the mourner into a journey of experiencing his honest fears and pains, hoping that by his emotional presence and counseling skills he will be helping him not to be overwhelmed, he will be helping him to weather the storm.

He too is buffeted by the storm. Who wouldn't be? But through his personal example of not flinching and by staying on course he demonstrates to his fellow passenger the possibility of enduring and not despairing. The function of the bereavement counselor is to be the fellow traveler who does not succumb to the fears and shadows of the valley. His attitude of patient endurance can transmit authentic hope more healthily than "words of wisdom."

The eight-session limit helps the counselor to control his countertransference feelings, which are normal and to be expected under the circumstances, but which must be kept in rein if the mourner (and the counselor) are ultimately to weather the storm.

In summary, the limit of eight counseling sessions is an integral part of the special design upon which the efficacy of Pastoral Bereavement Counseling is based. It is recommended in order to guard against the possible emergence of two dynamic processes that, if allowed to develop unimpeded, could weaken the effectiveness of the counseling.

The limit of eight sessions seeks to curtail the production of excessive client dependence and to control counselor countertransference. The special nature of bereavement counseling tends to stimulate the arousal of both these phenomena, and therefore the eight-session limit should be strictly followed.

THE COUNSELOR'S GOAL

At first, the goal seemed to be very simple—just to help the mourner. And perhaps it was better that way, without any preconceived notion of a more specific goal. It was important to let the mourners speak for themselves, to bare what was on their hearts without my pointing them in any particular direction. But I see now that I was able to chart a specific course for myself and for other counselors only after a pattern emerged.

I began to see that most bereaved persons, as they were freely expressing their feelings during counseling sessions, were experiencing common emotions and similar perplexities. They were hoping to be relieved of their emotional pain and to be restored to their previous level of functioning.

Most mourners described their loneliness, sadness, emotional and somatic pain, anger—their search for meaning and their being afflicted by feelings of guilt. They recounted their dysfunctions at home or on the job, in solitude and in their relationships. They wondered if they were going crazy, and feared that their apparent emotional weakness and inability to cope would become permanent disabilities.

"Will I ever get better? How am I going to face the future? What's going to become of me?"

Anyone who undertakes to share such feelings with a bereaved person, to listen and to stay with them for an hour—which was what I had offered to do—will quickly recognize that advice and preachment will not take them through the hour. The bereaved person is not helped by such an approach.

At the least, it may turn the mourner off—he realizes that the counselor has little empathy and has no genuine interest in "listening." At the worst, the mourner will feel angry and rejected. In instances where he represses his hurt because of timidity in the face of the clergyperson's rank, he may silently resent being stifled and dominated. He may vaguely feel this rejection as a fresh bereavement and as yet another loss while he is still smarting from the pain of his original loss.

I was very soon alerted to this danger by colleagues and mentors in the field of pastoral counseling, and I quickly eschewed even a hint of preaching. Instead, I instinctively resorted to other counseling techniques, such as "reflecting" and "identifying." It wasn't long before I realized that I had stumbled upon *the* technique that was most helpful, the means most appropriate for the *opening phases of counseling a mourner*.

Aside from the technical validity of such an approach, the mourner perceives such an attitude on the part of the counselor as *genuine empathy, as a readiness to listen, and as an encouragement to express his deepest feeling*.

In the bereaved person's state of being, casting about as

desperately as he is for some sign of genuine concern and support, the mourner's spirits begin to revive when he notices the counselor's resonances with the pain in his heart. He feels inner relief and a resurgence of hope.

Whether he formulates this perception clearly or vaguely, he recognizes that his prayers are being answered, that, just possibly, there may be a glimmer of light at the end of the darkness. I remember how stirred I was when I felt this happening during my early attempts at bereavement counseling. I can assure prospective bereavement counselors that they make look forward to a similar experience.

I remember feeling that a new world was opening up to me, richer and more intense than any other ministerial or pastoral counseling situation I had entered. A new opportunity for empathic encounter, for sharing a deep wrestling, a genuine and honest way of rendering an effective service to a human being in distress, was now in prospect.

This of course was only the first step in formulating the principles of Pastoral Bereavement Counseling; but it introduced me to the concept that the process of adjustment to grief is a *journey through a sequence of emotional states*. The journey is comprised of two stages:

1. The mourner needs to be made aware of his deep feelings; and,
2. If and when he completes an intense "working through" of all the emotional stages, he will feel completely healed.

The task of the Pastoral Bereavement Counselor is to allow (in some instances, encourage) the mourner to be in touch with his true and deep feelings, to support him as he moves through and endures the accompanying pain, to guide him over whatever obstacles may be blocking the "working through" process, and to "stay with" him till the journey is completed.

The formulation of the goal of Pastoral Bereavement Counseling should reflect this sense of counselor and mourner embarking together upon a journey, of being partners in a process. It should embody a joint commitment, but also reflect the practical constraints of the limited available time.

We therefore recommend that our counselors accept the

following statement as defining the target towards which they should direct their skill, empathy, time, and energy:

The goal of Pastoral Bereavement Counseling is to help the mourner take the first steps in the process of a healthy adjustment to his grief.

This goal is necessary and sufficient, it is both the minimum and the maximum. If the counselor aims for less, the whole enterprise becomes meagre and unworthy. If he stretches to do more, the counselor may be judged immodest and unrealistic, inappropriately vain and responsible for risking failure.

Taking the mourner through the "first steps" is significant and worthy. We see this as a true pioneering effort. It is significant because it has never been envisioned as a community service before, or as a dimension of pastoral ministry.

It is sufficient because to attempt a wider goal is to diffuse the concentration required to reach the "first steps" goal, especially critical for the mourner as he enters the bereavement process.

The "first steps" goal is neither simple nor easy. If it were, someone else would have packaged it long ago. It is a worthy and worthwhile challenge. It is a limited step with unlimited potential.

Presenting the Program to the Community

After clergy and/or others have been recruited and trained to become Pastoral Bereavement Counselors—a process which takes between 12 and 18 months, a community can commence to deliver support services. The Commission on Pastoral Bereavement Counseling, which has directed the introduction of this service into the New York metropolitan area, would be pleased to offer suggestions or guidance to any community that requests it.

1. *Announce the Availability of a New Support Service for Mourners*

Releases should be inserted in local news and communication media, advising that a new program is being offered by clergy and/or other public health volunteers. This support service is intended for people who have suffered the death of a loved one and are experiencing difficulty in the post-funeral period. Church, synagogue, and congregational bulletins, family agency and mental health agency newsletters should use similar copy. Funeral homes, hospitals, hospices, and nursing homes may disseminate the information through their public relations channels and institutional announcements.

The publicity material should always credit the sponsoring organizations or agencies, and should note that the program is being introduced on a nondenominational basis. It should be made clear that there are no fees charged, and that the program offers a limited number of sessions. "For those seeking further information, please contact _____, or call _____ ."

The copy should be neutral and should not place a premium on a response. There should be no aggressive promotion, and no guarantees of positive results. It is an announcement, not an advertisement. We aim to elicit responses that are self-initiated and self-filtered. We want to increase the probability that those mourners who respond and ask for help are the ones most likely to be benefited by the program.

Sample releases that have been used by the commission in New York* are available upon request from the publisher.

2. Set Up an Office for Coordination

One of the participating agencies should be designated to receive the initial calls and to provide first-line information. A central office is needed to assign cases to the counselors, to receive their reports for supervision, to team up counselors and supervisors, to establish locally applicable procedures for referrals to continued therapy when needed, and to conduct peer support groups for the interns and counselors.

---

*See the Appendix for a brief history of the commission.

3. Include a Supervisory Process

Pastoral Bereavement Counselors, whether clergy or from other helping professions, will need to be assured of responsible back-up personnel as they venture into the community to perform their sacred mission. With the best of intentions and with the greatest dedication to the application of counseling skills, counselors will need clinical supervision—to hone their skills, and as a dependable resource when unexpected problems arise.

It would be irresponsible for community leadership to rely on sincerity and altruism alone. Provision for supervision of the ongoing counseling is an integral part of the whole system, and no community should go forward with this enterprise until arrangements for proper supervision are in place.

In our work in the New York area, which we hope will be regarded as a pilot project upon which other communities may model their efforts, we are developing a supervisory plan that is less time-consuming than the fieldwork practicum that is usually utilized for the education of social workers and pastoral counselors.

We have designed a written form as a "Report for Supervision" that is especially useful for bereavement counseling, and that enables the counselor to record the pertinent data emerging in each session. The supervisors—who are also dedicated volunteers—lead group workshops, and are available by phone for guidance and problem solving.

We have recruited our volunteer supervisors from the chaplaincy and social work departments in major hospitals, staff members of mental health agencies, and private professionals who are interested in helping. Biweekly group sessions are arranged for the counselor-interns where mourners' case histories and verbatims are presented and discussed.

4. Sources of Funding

At our movement's present stage of development, it is probably best to solicit contributions from local sources in the community. Our New York effort has been funded by Special

Project Grants from the Federation of Jewish Philanthropies, The United Hospital Fund of New York, the New York Board of Rabbis, the Metropolitan Funeral Directors Association, several individual funeral homes, and a number of private benefactors.

We have also received a number of in-memoriam donations, as well as freewill offerings from mourners who were helped by our program. Many who have "graduated" from our counseling sessions have recommended the program to their friends in need, and a few have even expressed an interest in becoming counselors themselves.

Charitable and public service traditions vary from place to place; but each community will know best whom to approach to interest in this sort of project. The initiative can come from ministerial associations, or mental health agencies or the hospital-hospice institutions.

Under the auspices of an ad hoc committee, plans can be made for approaching funeral homes, business interests that wish to project a humanitarian public relations image, charitable and religious Foundations that aim to relieve emotional distress.

In all such requests for funding, it is important to stress that our movement aims to *deliver a much-needed service* to mourners. Our goal is not to proliferate conferences on death and dying, nor even to run a training course on bereavement, nor to raise consciousness on human mortality. Our goal is to set up, in each community that requests it, a functioning public mechanism that will support troubled mourners through a difficult hour of their lives, and bring them to a healthy healing.

We are convinced that our method is effective, that it facilitates a healthy—not painless—passage through the trauma. We've seen it make a difference in people's lives. We've seen them return to full functioning sooner than if they had faced their crisis unaided.

Arrangements for Continued Therapy, When Needed

Once we have extended a hand of support to the mourner, and even more so when he has reached out and grasped it, we cannot in good conscience lead him into a blind alley. We have a moral, ethical, and professional responsibility to design a framework for the program that will provide for referral to more intensive therapy, if necessary.

Therefore, while we fully expect that the large majority of mourner-clients who will be served by our program will be helped in eight sessions or less, we need to recognize that some will require more.

It does not matter what constitutes the dynamic source of this need. It sometimes arises from the nature of the therapeutic interaction. It may be due to deep-seated biases or neuroses that the mourner had been carrying within him for a long time, and which the shock of loss triggered off. It can become evident in bereavement counseling when lifetime patterns of defensive suppression of emotions may obstruct the channel to the mourner's deep emotions, which he needs to enter and to navigate through to reach a safe harbor.

It can be seen where a son or daughter, grieving for a parent from whom they've never completely separated as part of their adult individuation, struggles with the unfinished business that erupts in the wake of the stark and irreversible separation by death. Sometimes, when the mourner is hysterical, unable to put even a temporary cap on an outpouring of relentless emotion, the journey cannot be completed in eight sessions.

Whatever the dynamic explanation in particular cases, it is the responsibility of those who wish to introduce Pastoral Bereavement Counseling into their communities to arrange opportunities for more intensive therapy as an integral part of their program. In most communities, the mental health agencies or family counseling services would be suitable for accepting such referrals, and would be in a position to implement whatever professional long-term therapy might be required.

The manner of referral within the context of the eight original sessions is also an issue that our counselors should ponder. The 12-hour training course includes instructions on how the counselor should proceed in making the counselee aware of his need for further therapy.

Identifying Mourners Who Need Further Therapy

Another advantage of our structured design is that it enables a would-be Pastoral Bereavement Counselor to enter into this activity with confidence. A clergyperson, or any volunteer for that matter, will not think of himself as an expert in psychiatric diagnosis. Even though his goal is to journey through only the "first steps," he may be concerned as to how to recognize potential damage to the counselee in time to refer him to competent treatment.

In most cases, our counselors will not be fully trained psychiatrists or psychologists. While their intentions will certainly be of the best, a situation may arise where their involvement might unwittingly cause a delay in bringing to proper attention an underlying problem that requires intensive treatment.

There are three elements in our program's design that guard against this possibility. The first is that, as we have recommended, the program should not be aggressively promoted; it should only be announced as available. For a mourner who recognizes, or whose family and friends recognize, that grief has propelled him into an extremely frightening emotional state, our program is clearly not the answer and our offer of availability will probably not be accepted.

If, despite our low-key announcement, appropriate help is not sought and such a "close to the brink" griever does choose us, we will at least be in a position of a trusted door-opener who will be able to direct the troubled mourner to the intensive therapy he needs. The Pastoral Bereavement Counselor will then have had an indispensable share in the eventual rehabilitation of that bereaved individual.

The second safeguard is the built-in accompaniment of supervision, even in the limited manner we've suggested. While a Pastoral Bereavement Counselor may not recognize some subtle manifestations of incipient pathology, or may not be able to diagnose them with certainty, we can expect that the supervisor will. At the least, our program will have fulfilled its responsibility by recommending further treatment.

The third safeguard that has been designed into the structure is the limited number of sessions and the goal of taking the "first steps." This interjects a sense of "journeying" and a structure of movement into the proceedings. The counselor aims to take the mourner through "the *first steps*" of mourning, implying a recognition that there are further "steps" ahead. Equally, the mourner, by his commitment to a number of sessions, implies his understanding that he is engaged in a *journey* marked by travel and *progress through emotions*.

The contract, the concentration, the dynamic purpose and process of the proceedings between counselor and counselee, the hope and expectations that animate the counseling exchanges, the flow of emotional expression—all combine to convey a sense of movement toward a change in the mourner's life. The very fact of scheduling appointments from week to week confirms an expectation of progress.

And usually, progress and change do take place. At first slowly and ever so subtly, the mourner begins to experience movement in his feelings. They are as painful as ever, troublesome and disconcerting, but they are not exactly the same.

The mourner doesn't openly acknowledge the slight change. Even after the counselor tentatively points to it, the mourner will often deny that *any* change has taken place.

But when the different qualify of feeling takes hold—even a slight difference—when it is undeniably real; the mourner can be brought toward direct recognition. He can begin to take ungrudging notice of the progress. *This is often the turning point of the therapy*.

The design of Pastoral Bereavement Counseling that produces this recognition of change can be used as a benchmark in determining which mourners may need counseling beyond the usual eight sessions. A useful rule of thumb is:

Additional therapy is to be recommended when there is no change in the mourner's feelings, as he reports them during the eight counseling sessions.

If the mourner is expressing the same feelings in the fourth session as he was in the first, and if he's reporting the same behavior patterns in the fifth, sixth, and seventh sessions, the counselor should recommend continued counseling with another agency or therapist.

The structure of Pastoral Bereavement Counseling as we have outlined in this chapter, makes it possible to introduce this beneficial program for mourners in a responsible and accountable manner. The method is highly effective because it provides a framework for a purposeful and therapeutic relationship between two consenting adults, in a manner that enables it to be endorsed by community organizations, using counseling approaches that are based upon actual clinical experience, and that reckon with the relevant clinical issues.

Chapter 5

COUNSELING SKILLS APPROPRIATE TO THE MOURNER'S FEELINGS

In bereavement counseling a technique is more than a technical matter. Bereavement counselors expose, touch, and engage with the most emotion-laden subject in our human experience. They will fail if they act coldly, if they act only as technicians.

The appropriate technical skills must be understood, of course, their importance appreciated, their timing chosen by using our critical intelligence. But their application at times of bereavement should flow from a deep sensitivity, from a pervasive "feeling with," from an ever-present commitment to offer "heart and mind" for the healing of the mourner.

The willingness of a would-be counselor to undertake actual counseling sessions can be tested by asking him to imagine himself immersed in the mourner's world. Such an exercise can function not only as an assessment of a counselor's future dedication, but also as a preparation for infusing every application of technique with utmost sensitivity. In bereavement counseling, a callous application of technique can seriously impede a mourner's progress.

Empathy, like love, can be experimented with in one's

imagination before it is consummated in the flesh. Both intimacies are prepared for by prior exercises of allowing oneself to imagine how they would feel in the actual act.

I therefore feel it best to divide our discussion of "technique" into three parts:

1. The mourner's feelings during bereavement, and the pattern of progression of these feelings, as we have noted them in clinical experiences;
2. The dynamic explanations for these apparently natural and universal feelings and for the sequence they appear to follow;
3. A therapeutic response to heal those feelings.

This chapter will discuss the mourner's feelings.

Our Pastoral Bereavement Counselors should not expect to encounter *all* of these feelings in every counseling situation. Individual mourners in the community who will avail themselves of our services will be responding at different stages of their mourning process and with differing perceptions of their needs. Also, not every mourner passes through *all of these stages* with equal or similar intensities.

Occasionally, some of these feelings appear to be bypassed altogether. But, based upon our clinical experience of counseling more than 500 mourners, the usual feelings of mourners can be grouped under six categories:

> Sadness
> Numbness and denial
> Mild dysfunction
> Illusory thinking
> Anger
> Guilt

It should be understood that this listing of the emotions of grief is only for purposes of conceptual clarity. In actual counseling they are rarely encountered in such a neat frame or specific order. They frequently overlap, are rarely expressed without ambivalence, and never change in one direction only.

The mourner's feelings are usually not on an even keel. They fluctuate back and forth, registering progress, obstruction, or regression. Sometimes, the mourner's emotions seem to be standing still for weeks at a time.

Yet, whatever stage the counselor encounters, he should empathize with what the mourner has already endured, and with what he can anticipate to be lying ahead. He would do well to consciously invite this knowledge to bear upon his selection of appropriate technique, and the manner of application.

The counselor's *heart* needs to "know" the mourner's feelings so that his empathy may be strengthened and replenished. The counselor's *mind* needs to "know" the mourner's feelings so that he may identify the particular stage of the mourner's grief and be able to gauge the direction and pace of the mourner's journeyings.

SADNESS

The mourner feels lost, alone and afraid, cut off and adrift. The bedrock support he or she felt for many years is suddenly gone.

He wants to cry, but cultural and psychosocial pressures impede unrestricted release of emotion. She wants to cry but fears she may not be able to stop. He feels weak and helpless, but can't allow himself to show it. She can't imagine life without him, she feels helpless and hopeless.

"I can't lift myself out of my sadness. What's wrong with me?"

"I miss him so much, I cry and can't stop crying."

"I think of nothing else except that I've lost her."

"Will I ever love again?"

"I just do things automatically, no zest, all the flavor is gone."

"I have nothing to look forward to—part of me inside is dead."

"I see people laughing and I say to myself that I'll never laugh again."

"I see couples holding hands and I burst into tears."

"I can't concentrate on anything."

"I sit in front of the television but I don't see the picture."

"It's terrible, I'm lonely, I'm sad, I'm scared."

"Sometimes I want to die."

"I have no appetite. I just dawdle and pick at the food. I don't eat but I don't feel hungry."

"I'm gaining weight. I snack all day."

"I don't ever feel comfortable in any place. I have to get out of the house. I walk for blocks staring straight ahead. I can't sit still."

"For me it's all over, I have no future."

"I'm just plain sad, I'm sorry for myself. I wander around, I don't enjoy anything."

"I miss him very much. Our lives were intertwined. Now that he's gone I have no purpose."

"I'm not living, I'm just existing."

"One day is like another."

"The nights are just dreadful, long and lonely and no relief."

"I don't want anything except to survive. I'm not even sure I want that."

Expressions of sadness often join, gradually and subtly, with feelings of anger. For example: "I don't enjoy life any more, it has no meaning. Tell me, what's the meaning of life anyway? It makes no sense, it's so unfair! I don't understand it, it's cruel and unjust! He worked hard for forty years, and never lived to enjoy the fruit of his labors. Now he's gone and he's spoiled it for me too. I'm all alone, I can't enjoy. I'm screaming inside—Why!? Why!?"

In such a case, the counselor chooses to focus on *one or the other* of the feelings, depending upon the *stage of the therapy* and the *readiness of the client* to accept an intervention. Usually, he will want to bring the mourner to identify his "sadness" before helping him to recognize his "anger."

NUMBNESS AND DENIAL

For the mourner the pain is so sharp, so harsh and cruel, that it cannot be directly confronted, much less assimilated. It can be approached only in a limited and hesitant fashion. The counselor needs to understand this, and to empathize with the mourner's difficulties.

It is unrealistic to expect the mourner to quickly and directly acknowledge his terror. He can move toward an acknowledgment of his pain and loss only through a circuitous route. What we label as numbness and denial are the perfect aids, the special eyeglasses, that nature manufactures for our emotional vision to help us "feel" our way through a difficult experience.

The numbness dulls the sharpness of the shock, the denial delays the painful confrontation with reality. Without these merciful distortions of perception, the mourner would find his early movements through grief to be not even barely bearable.

> Sometimes I don't believe he's really dead. I know we buried him, I was there, I saw it with my own eyes—yet, at the same time, I just don't know, maybe he went to sleep, maybe he'll wake up and come back to me. What's wrong with me? I know it sounds crazy, but sometimes I have these thoughts—sometimes I start hoping so strongly—I just don't know—I'm all mixed up.

Fluctuations between acceptance and denial, gingerly movement toward facing reality, emotional confusion, a jumble of disparate and opposing feelings—these are what most mourners go through as part of the normal process of bereavement.

But these are also what most mourners never get a chance to express, nor even to become aware of within themselves. More's the pity, because the fuller the awareness, the healthier would be the resolution of the grief.

Mourners are able to express such sentiments only in a setting that encourages open expression of feelings, where the client feels safe in uttering even seemingly bizarre thoughts, where the purpose—stated or understood—is therapeutic. This is precisely what the structured sessions in Pastoral Bereavement Counseling aim to offer, and what informal conversations with mourners have heretofore not been able to provide.

Many of the mourners we have counseled in our New York program have expressed this kind of partial denial. It appears as though their perceptions temporarily operates on a split level.

One part of them can acknowledge the cruel reality. Another part of their consciousness imagines that the worst is not final, that a reprieve is still possible.

Even though these thoughts are logical opposites, the mourner feels them fully, existentially, *and simultaneously*. Their presence in tight tandem in the mourner's stream of consciousness produces a powerful and violent discomfort, made more frightening by its very vagueness, its complexity and inexpressibility.

Indirect Indications of Denial

Often the mourner's denial is indicated only in a roundabout manner. The counselor then needs to listen carefully and empathize deeply in order to discern the indirect indications, before he can attempt to bring the mourner to self-recognition.

For example, he may notice that the mourner always speaks of his beloved's death euphemistically, using such phrases as:

"He passed away."

"He breathed his last."

"He didn't wake up."

"He closed his eyes and didn't open them."

"She slipped away peacefully."

"He left this earth."

"She came to her peace."

"She was taken away."

"He went to Heaven."

When this is the *only* way the mourner refers to the beloved's death, it usually signifies that the mourner is in some measure denying the full reality. Of course, we are not recommending that the grief-stricken mourner should be forced into uttering the stark words, "My beloved has died."

But when the counselor notices a consistent pattern of avoidance of the word "death," it should alert him to a central therapeutic task to which he will need to give his attention. The mourner will need to move toward a diminished fantasizing about his situation, and the counselor is in a position to facilitate that movement.

"What was that last phrase you used? How did you describe what happened to Marvin? Do you remember the words you just now used?"

"I said, 'Marvin passed away.' "

"Is that correct? You're expressing yourself in a certain way. Let me try to understand what you're saying. Tell me again, what happened to Marvin?"

"Why is a certain word so important?"

"Well, because you've never used it. This is our third hour, and you and I know what we're here for, we both know what's happened in your life, but I don't hear you saying it clearly. Maybe it's your way of partially denying what's happened."

"No. I know that Marvin passed away. He won't come back."

"Why not? Why can't he come back?"

"Oh, I wish he could. I miss him so, I need him, I'm so lonely without him."

"Shh, shh, say it quietly. Why won't Marvin come back? I know it's hard to speak it, say it softly. What happened to Marvin? Why can't he come back?"

There ensued a long pause. Clearly, the widow was struggling with her feelings. The counselor leaned forward in a supportive gesture and spoke intently. "Marvin can't come back because he—."

"Because he—died. Is that what you want me to say?"

"It's true, isn't it? Marvin can't come back because he's dead. I'm sorry for the pain, but I think you should hear it directly—and be able to speak it directly. That's one of the ways we're trying to help you. Marvin died. It's better if you say it directly. It's the truth, isn't it? Marvin was sick and he died—and you're mourning for him."

Later, at the conclusion of therapy, this widow remembered this exchange as a turning point that helped her to "work through" her denial and move on to other stages of feeling.

Another example of an indirect indication of remaining too long in the stage of denial is when the mourner reports an obsession with the remains of the body in the grave or with preoccupation with where the spirit is. (This could be an indication of repressed guilt, as well.)

If this is part of the mourner's casual concerns, it can be considered normal for the early stages. But when the mourner is fixated on this issue, the counselor needs to consider the possibility that the mourner is still in the stage of denial.

"This is our fourth session, and you're asking once again what's happening to your mother's body in the earth. What are you feeling about it?"

"I don't like to imagine it. I think it's terrible. What's happening to my beautiful mother? She was always so well-groomed. How long does it take for . . . it . . . to change?"

"I don't know. But why is this important to you?"

"Because I can't bear the thought that she died."

"Are you wishing that her body could remain the way it was? Unchanged?"

"Maybe."

"Maybe it's hard for you to let her go and to face the fact that her body is buried in the earth. There's a kind of finality to that thought, and perhaps that's what you're finding so difficult."

"But I know that she died."

"You know and you don't know. Part of you recognizes the full consequences of her death, and part of you is still struggling with the finality of what happened. Your *mind* knows that she was buried in a grave, but your *heart* is uncomfortable when you imagine it, so you keep asking questions about it."

"You mean, if I fully understand that my mother died and if I fully understand that she's buried, I'll be less worried about what's happening?"

"It might be like that. It's hard to accept the harsh facts. It's pretty normal to know and to fight against knowing, at the same time."

"I'm glad to hear that you think I'm pretty normal."

Denial may be encountered directly or indirectly, or noticed as a phenomenon of general numbness in the mourner's emotional life. In whichever form it is observed, the counselor has a role to play in helping the mourner travel through this stage.

Numbness

This state of feeling is frequently seen at some point during the early stages of adjustment to grief. It is an involuntary but natural mechanism that offers some protection from too-sudden immersion into the harshness and sharpness of loss. It temporarily shields the mourner from the psychological perplexity arising from the tension and ambivalence of opposite feelings.

Numbness allows the mourner to undertake an indirect tentative approach to the fullness of his pain. It mercifully delays the full impact of meeting the trauma head-on. It provides a mechanism for the mourner to move into his personal "valley of the shadow" at his own pace and speed.

The principal danger is when the numbness becomes too severe or too prolonged. It is part of the counselor's task to monitor the pace of its deepening or waning. The 8-week sequence in which Pastoral Bereavement Counseling takes place is a useful time frame during which the extent and direction of the mourner's numbness can be evaluated.

What are the signs the counselor should look for?   Symptoms to note are a pattern of dullness in the mourner's routine activities, and a flatness or lethargy in the mourner's descriptions of his emotional experiences. Our clinical experience indicates that the quality of numbness is more accurately measured through attention to non-mourning activities than to the mourner's interior feelings that we have been describing till now.

We have found it very useful to look for an opportunity, during the first few sessions, to pose this kind of question:

"What did you do today?" or
"What have you been doing in the past few days?"
Such an inquiry may serve two purposes:

1. It can help the counselor to gauge the level of the mourner's numbness and lethargy;
2. It can serve as a key to unlock the door to expression of deeply felt emotion.

In response, the mourner will talk about the activities that are occupying his time and attention, and the counselor may obtain some data from which he may be able to estimate the extent of the mourner's numbness, if it is present in the situation.

In response to this question, the mourner may report on

such activities as job performance, business decisions, interpersonal contacts, health concerns, eating and sleeping patterns, family relationships, financial transactions, disposition of the deceased's clothes, and consultations about the estate.

In listening to the mourner's description of his usual routine, the counselor seeks to gauge the depth or shallowness of emotional intensity. In this instance, the counselor is not listening to the *content* of the material as much as he is watching for the accompanying *affect* and *manner*. The counselor should be wondering:

"How appropriate is the mourner's emotional involvement, or lack of it, in connection with the words that are being spoken? Are the mourner's emotions, as he is describing the events of his routine, in consonance with the situation being described, or does he seem detached from feeling?"

For example, a widow of 4 months was describing her tendency to procrastinate and put off the task of sorting out her deceased husband's clothes. "I know I should get to it, but I keep on postponing opening his closet door, I just can't do it."

"It's difficult and painful, isn't it?"

"It's like saying the final goodbye. Every time I pass the door and know his clothes are on the rack, it's as though part of him is still in the house with me. Once I take the clothes out, he won't be home anymore. Nothing, I'll be alone."

The words are emotion-laden, but her manner was flat and even, without intonation, with no rising or lowering of inflection. Her eyes stared straight ahead. Her mind was in touch with the situation, but her heart was numb and unfeeling. Her automatic manner and lethargic affect was the visible symptom of her interior emotional numbness. She had distanced herself—in feeling—from the pain of confronting her loss by shrinking from the logical necessity of disposing of her husband's clothes.

What I witnessed was a process that had begun with a flight from pain through the mechanism of "denial," and which was being transformed into a generalized deadening of feeling. A mourner's numbness is the symptomatic result of the weakening of emotional vigor which, originally utilized for the purpose of avoiding pain, broadens into a weakening in other emotional areas as well. As the psychiatrist in the movie *Ordi-*

nary People says to the troubled surviving brother, "If you can't feel pain, you can't feel anything else."

How does the counselor move the mourner out of numbness and towards restored emotional vigor? By leading the mourner out of the false security and counterproductiveness of "denial." As the griever moves closer to facing the reality of living without his beloved—with more pain, but also with the support of the counselor's empathy and therapeutic guidance—he will begin to feel restored in other emotional areas as well.

This course was successfully implemented in this instance of the widow of 4 months. A few weeks later she reported that she had opened the closet, sorted out her husband's clothes, and donated them to charity.

MILD DYSFUNCTION

Like numbness, the behavioral (or somatic) dysfunctions that many mourners experience are symptoms that the counselor should note but not expect to directly alleviate. They may be regarded as signposts along the road to either recovery or regression.

As the journey progresses through the stages of mourning, these symptoms usually dissipate. If the counselor notes these behaviors remaining constant throughout the eight sessions, or markedly intensifying, he should consider that they may signal a need for continuing therapy.

Some of the dysfunctions that mourners complain of are outlined in the following sections.

Withdrawal

This is an overt pattern of behavior, more conscious than not, through which the mourner tries to flee from the pain of losing and the sadness of being lost. The mourner runs away from life itself, because every aspect of living reminds him of what once was and is no longer.

"What did you do yesterday?"

"I don't remember. I didn't do very much. I'm so sad I just want to be left alone. I'd rather not go out in the street. I don't want to meet anyone, or talk, or be reminded. . . ."

Another typical response was, "When I got up in the morning I didn't even want to go to work. I finally did go, but I left the office early. I don't want to make any decisions. I just want to be left alone, I don't want to look at anyone. I guess I just want to mope the day away—sometimes I think I'm becoming a recluse."

Frantic Automatic Activity

The mourner throws himself into an endless pattern of busyness, flitting from one activity to another, trying to stave off and to push away an emotional engagement with pain. This strategy is really a covert withdrawal, a hiding behind a facade of zest, a frenzied effort to "hear no evil, see no evil." The mourner is driven to deny, to escape, to pretend a heightened normalcy. The pattern may begin as a conscious device but can regress into a largely unconscious reflexive activity.

"What did you do yesterday?"

"Oh, I'm doing all right. I'm keeping very busy, I don't have time to think. I have many friends, and they're always inviting me out. My job keeps me very busy, and I have no time to think about missing Al. I have so many things to do. I hardly have time to take a shower. Even the weekends are busy, I'll never stay home alone, I'm doing all right."

Irritability

Some mourners go through periods of impoliteness and impatience. A personality pattern that had been mild and docile suddenly becomes snappy and belligerent. Family, neighbors, coworkers may notice an abrasiveness.

They may respond to the mourner's unexpected rudeness by arguing with him or shunning his company, either course resulting in the mourner's increased isolation. This in turn generates more frustration, anger, and self-pity, and the mourner can become even more rude.

Somatic Disturbances

Sometimes, the feelings of worry, irritability, and incipient anger become connected with physical symptoms—tiredness, vague pains, stomach discomfort, headaches, and nervousness. (It should be noted that Pastoral Bereavement Counselors do not give medical advice. If they feel a doctor's intervention might be advisable, they should suggest it to the mourner).

Sometimes there are changes in living patterns, in either direction. The mourner may complain of insomnia (which may be due to emotional agitation), or of too much sleeping (withdrawal or depression). He may be eating more (avoiding and escaping) or less (guilt, self-punishment or depression).

If the counselor encounters any of these, his task is to note the presence of the symptoms, to make a general estimate of their meaning—his main function is to be supportive and not analytic—and to be alert for changes in these symptoms as the counseling proceeds.

His main purpose is to encourage *movement* through the emotional sequences that are characteristic of the process of adjusting to a loss. A lessening of symptomatic intensity is a sure sign that the movement is proceeding healthily.

Preoccupation with the Loss

Mourners may express their fears and concerns in this fashion:

"I can't think of anything else day or night. I go around all the time remembering and reliving. I can't forget that phone call telling me that he was being rushed from the office to the hospital. That was the beginning of the nightmare. I can't shut off the nightmare. It was terrible, I'm still perplexed and confused—and alone. I try to put my attention to something else, but the memory and the emptiness never goes away. I can't clean the house, I can't talk on the phone without crying, I can't balance the checkbook. I can't keep Irving out of my mind. It's months now and I should be getting over it, but all I can think of is, 'Irving, Irving, Where are you?' Am I going out of my mind? Will it ever end?"

Inability to Concentrate

"My work in the office is shot to pieces. I find my mind wandering even in the middle of a telephone call. I think of her, and wonder how I'm going to raise the kids. As you know, I'm an accountant, but lately I'm losing my place in the column of figures, right in the middle of using the calculator. I can't concentrate on anything at home. Even after the kids are in bed, I sit at my desk and try to catch up on my work, I can't keep my mind on it. I'm worried I'm going to lose some clients."

Or, another example:

"Tell me what you did yesterday."

"It's no use—I couldn't do anything. Almost the whole day was wasted on nothing. I was in the house all the time. I had no place for myself, I walked around and cried. I tried to clean the living room.

"Do you know how long it took me to water the plants? I'm ashamed to tell you, there must be something wrong with me. Do you know how long it took me to water the plants?—Two-and-a-half hours!—I couldn't even do a simple thing like that! I just couldn't keep my mind on it. I can't go on this way, I really have to take hold of myself."

"You really think of him all the time, don't you? Instead of two and a half hours, how long should it take?"

"To do what?"

"To water the plants."

"It used to take me ten minutes. It's so simple, and I used to get such pleasure out of it, but I just couldn't keep my mind on it. I can't concentrate anymore—on anything."

"Your loss and pain are taking up all your emotional energy. It's very hard to go through this. I'm very sorry for your pain."

"When will it end? Will it ever end?"

"I hope so. We're trying. We're going to keep on trying."

A few sessions later this widow casually reported that she had watered the plants in a half hour.

Daydreaming

Sometimes the mourner will take refuge from his pain and disturbing feelings by daydreaming in an almost conscious and deliberate fashion. The mourner seems to opt for a pleasant avoidance. He knows that the scene that he is imagining is unreal and inauthentic, yet he needs to choose an emotional respite from his constant unremitting trauma.

Daydreaming can be understood as a variation of the same psychological process that produces numbness and denial. It is to the need to be temporarily shielded from shock and pain.

If the counselor sees it as temporary and within the mourner's control, he should not consider it as basically unhealthy. Of course, if the mourner shows signs of adopting daydreaming as the primary coping mechanism for all his stresses, the counselor must recognize this as incipient pathology.

"What did you do yesterday?"

"Nothing very much. I missed him and cried when I thought of him. You know, sometimes I feel myself smiling when I think of him, how is that possible?"

"What exactly were you remembering?"

"I was imagining that he was on his way home to me from work, that he's coming around the corner and in five minutes will ring the bell downstairs. I was so happy even though I knew it was a dream."

"I can understand that it made you happy. Are there any other thoughts—or imaginings—that make you happy that you can tell me about?"

"Sometimes I don't know whether to cry or to just run away and dream. Sometimes I imagine that I'm far away from all of this. I fantasize that I'm on a cruise to Mexico, that Sam is with me, that we're dining together by candlelight, and that we're walking together on the ship's deck gazing out on a moonlit sea. I know it's only a dream, and when I'll rouse myself awake I'll burst into tears all over again. But for a few minutes it was worth it."

"And you get a little peace from that kind of dream."

"I'm sorry if I'm doing wrong, but sometimes I feel that I just can't go on moping and being angry and sad. Is it wrong? Is it crazy?"

"Other people who are suffering also go through some imaginings like that. For now I think it's okay, and if you continue to have these imaginings it's all right if you tell me about them."

Procrastination

Bereavement may bring about alterations in a mourner's style of living and of meeting problems. A mourner may recognize that he has become consciously lethargic and less ambitious. He has more to worry about, but less zest to undertake any action.

"I can't seem to get anything done. I know I've got to make an appointment to see the dentist, but each week I put it off till the next. What's the point of hurrying? For me life is over anyway. You know, for two months my sister has been after me to talk to the lawyer. I know I'll have to do it sooner or later, but I just keep postponing it. I'm postponing everything these days, and I once was such a methodical and ambitious person. Everything had to be neat and in place. Now I've become sloppy and lazy, and just want to crawl into my hole. My response to everyone's advice is, 'You're right, but I can't do it today, I'll do it tomorrow.'"

To sum up: The Pastoral Bereavement Counselor can expect to hear mourners report some behavioral dysfunctions, and/or some somatic changes or distress. In most cases, these will not need to be "reflected" back to the client as a therapeutic intervention, although the counselor's notice of them is seen by the mourner as further evidence of the counselor's genuine empathy.

We will see later that the counselor's "reflection" of other feelings—sadness, anger, or guilt—has a more significant therapeutic purpose.

It is important that the counselor pay attention to patterns of dysfunction because they may then be used as a benchmark, among other signs, with which to measure the mourner's improvement, or regression, or fixation during the course of the counseling.

When these symptoms lessen it is usually a sign of wholesome movement towards healing. When these symptoms persist throughout the eight sessions, both counselor and supervisor will need to consider referral for additional therapy.

ILLUSORY THINKING

It is not unusual for a mourner to enter into a temporary emotional state that combines daydreaming and denial and that moves towards hallucinatory episodes. The longing, the pain, the loneliness and perplexity can become so intense that relief is welcomed even at the cost of submitting to an irrational vision. Let me cite three examples from our case histories.

1. "At six o'clock I hear his key in the door. What's wrong with me? I talk to him. Sometimes he helps me balance the checkbook. I hear his voice and his expressions. Sometimes I stand by the window, wagering with myself that he'll come around the corner any second—the seventh one from now—the eleventh one from now."

2. "I'm ashamed to tell you this, I know a man isn't supposed to be a weakling and cry, but I miss her so much. I have a real need for her, and I don't know where to turn. Yesterday, at the office, in the middle of dictation, the tears welled up and I couldn't continue. I went into the men's room and luckily there was no one there and I burst out sobbing.

"Do you know how I calmed myself? I fantasized that I'd go back to my office and call her and say I'd meet her for dinner. I mused on this for about ten minutes and I was so happy that I actually picked up the phone and dialed. When my mother answered I was so shocked into reality that I dropped the phone.

"But for a few minutes there I was actually looking forward to talking with her. That night I woke up crying and found myself caressing her pillow, and I cried and talked to her and begged her to come back. Am I weak or crazy? Are they going to put me into an institution?"

3. One widow told of an incident on a hot summer day, 6 months after her husband's death. She was shopping in an air-conditioned store and suddenly was seized with a compulsion to go home and tell her husband not to go out into the hot street. She interrupted her shopping and walked two full blocks all the way to her apartment door, before recognizing and remembering that her husband was dead. Even then, she felt compelled to open the door to her apartment and look around for Henry, one part of her "knowing" how foolish all this was, and another part of herself reveling in the self-deception.

Generally, the counselor's response to these behaviors, especially if they are encountered in the early sessions is, "These seem to be your true and deep feelings. I'm glad that you're telling me so much about them."

ANGER

There are two other principal emotions experienced by the mourner that still remain to be described. Anger and guilt are different in quality and operate with greater pressure upon the mourner than the feelings mentioned up till now. They are more intensely felt and are more powerfully influential over the mourner's inner life than the others. They have greater control over the mourner than he has over them.

Anger and guilt are the primal and principal emotions in the experience of grief, and the toughest for the mourner to endure. They are the bedrock reactions to the inescapable fact of loss. No real movement towards wholesome healing is possible without an honest experience of passage through guilt and through anger.

Yet, anger and guilt are also—perhaps just *because* of their primary and painful nature—more deeply buried in the mourner's consciousness, and more likely to resist being uncovered in counseling.

In many cases the counselor will find that, while the mourner may quite easily be brought to acknowledge his feelings of sadness, denial, functional distress, and daydreaming, the same mourner will resist moving toward a recognition of his anger and guilt. The prospect of encountering these gut feelings can increase a mourner's fears and agitation.

Anger and guilt touch the mourner's spirit with greater violence and intensity than sadness; anger and guilt disturb the temporary peace artificially provided by numbness and denial; anger and guilt destroy the peaceful facade that can be produced by daydreaming. More than anything else, anger and guilt signal to the deepest recesses of the mourner's interior that he has lost control, and silently infuriate him toward a further sense of guilt.

A sane mourner *does feel anger* and *does experience guilt*, and at the same time is also *angry and guilty at what he is feeling and experiencing*. He is agitated because it seems to be getting worse, not better.

This fundamental tension can create empathic and technical difficulties for the counselor. His task is to help the mourner endure and "pass through" painful territory. He knows the journey is necessary and unavoidable, but he also empathically flinches from imposing and, in a sense, inflicting, pain. He understands that rational people logically seek to escape pain, not embrace it.

Yet, because he is a bereavement counselor, he realizes that the mourner is enmeshed in a nonlogical situation, and he with him. Because he is a bereavement counselor he realizes that there is no easy way, that avoidance and denial of problematic feelings only lead to a lengthier trauma.

Because he is a Pastoral Bereavement Counselor it is hoped that he will feel personally and clinically fortified by his faith that the map he is offering the mourner to navigate through this fearsome territory will provide a safe path—for himself and his client.

The primal tension that anger creates within the mourner—the feeling that he's been *cheated* and, *simultaneously*, his anger at feeling anger—often hinders clear recognition of this central emotion, and the part it plays in his journey.

Similarly, as we shall see in the next chapter, feelings of guilt are quite normal in the bereavement process. But because there are dynamic and cultural impediments to acknowledge guilt, the bereaved person cannot easily integrate a feeling of self-blame, and finds it difficult to "stay with" and "pass through" this emotion.

A self-engagement with anger and guilt are problematic for a mourner because there are inner resistances to acknowledging oneself that the self is out of control. In addition, the cultural ambience of our times exalts "macho" strength and regards any acknowledgment of emotional difficulty as a weakness.

In dealing with these gut feelings of the mourner, the counselor has a twofold task:

1. To help the mourner reach down to the core of his anger and guilt; and,
2. To help the mourner stay on course as he journeys through these emotions; to guide him so that his route is not deflected by their intensity or the discomfort they induce.

Some clinical examples of how mourners express anger are:

"How could God do this to me? I didn't even get a warning."

"We were so looking forward to retiring and enjoying life. Now—I have nothing."

"He worked so hard all his life!"

"Why didn't the doctor tell us to go to the hospital immediately?"

"It's so unfair!"

"What's the meaning of life, anyway!"

"I'm angry when I see bums on the street, and read about criminals. They're living and don't deserve to live—my husband was such a good man."

"I resent it when I see happy couples on the dance floor. I'm very jealous. We deserved it too. Why can't we have it?"

Frequently, when the counselor allows or encourages the mourner to ventilate his deep resentments, the mourner will declare anger at the deceased themselves: "How could Marvin do this to me?! He went and spoiled everything. He had no right to leave me alone!"

Or, the words of a father railing at a seventeen-year-old son who was killed while bicycling on a country road:

"How many times did I tell him to be careful, he just didn't listen. He was always headstrong and rebellious. He always knew better than anyone else! Now look what he did! How could he do this to me—to his mother, to all of us! How could God let him do it?! How can I believe, how can I pray?! I'll never go to church again—not for a long time."

Sometimes, the dynamic source of sadness and depression is anger or rage that has been suppressed. When deep emotions are acknowledged, when counseling permits these emotions to be released, the depression lightens.

As we will see from other excerpts, the mourner's anger can be directed at God, at the doctor, at fate, at the deceased, and even at the suffering mourner himself. It is not uncommon to witness the mourner expressing anger at his deficiencies, which become compulsively and illogically transformed into the cause that killed the beloved. The mourner feels anger, self-blame, and guilt—irrationally, compulsively, and painfully.

GUILT

A mourner who expresses guilt sees his emotions as logical and justified; he feels really guilty. He honestly believes he has done wrong, and cites chapter and verse to prove it. Indeed, the first tip-off to the counselor of the depth and intensity of the mourner's conviction that he is to blame, is the eagerness with which he talks about it. There is usually a pronounced breast-beating, an insistence that the listener *must* agree that the mourner is guilty. It is usually clear that the mourner is seeking expiation.

But the counselor needs to recognize that seeking to grant the mourner's wish by invoking logic and reality will not release the mourner from his compulsive, irrational guilt. An illogical pain cannot be alleviated by a logical appeal to reason.

First, the mourner has to allow himself to be wholeheartedly engaged in his emotional journey, to know clearly that he *is* wrestling. He needs to accept the give-and-take of the struggle with as much courage as he can muster. Logic can help; but only after the trauma has been at least partially endured and the journey through emotion at least partially traversed. A few clinical examples of mourner's expressions of guilt:

"Why did God punish me like this? What did I do wrong?"

"I should have let him retire."

"I shouldn't have let him retire."

"I should have told her I loved her more often."

"Why didn't I call the ambulance right away?"

"How can I enjoy living when she's in the grave?"

"I can't forgive myself for the first feeling I had when the hospital called to tell me my mother had finally died. I felt relief because her suffering was finally over."

A mourner's sense of guilt may be evident in ways other than through the spoken word. It can be recognized as a factor in a mourner's declining to move out of his sadness, or of holding on to a pattern of procrastination. It may even be an unconscious motive in the case of a griever refusing to avail himself of gratis bereavement counseling. Such a mourner may perceive of the extension of our helping hand as a thwarting of the punishment they vaguely feel they deserve.

In supportive bereavement counseling, as opposed to the analytic, the counselor's response to mourner's guilt is *only* to recognize it, to bring the mourner to identify and to perceive it clearly, and to guide the mourner in the process of "working it through." In most of the instances our Commission has dealt with, the counselor's attitude of consistent acceptance of all feelings and his implicit assurance that guilt is normal for bereaved persons, has facilitated this working-through process.

For the counselor to be able to assure a mourner of his essential "normalcy," it is essential that he himself acquire a clear understanding of the dynamics of the journey-through-grief process. Why do these feelings that we have described arise? What is their source, and their usual sequential connection?

The counselor is *with* the mourner empathically, but he is *apart* from the mourner in his role of monitoring and guiding the process. He will be able to function effectively insofar as he is familiar and comfortable with the unfolding stages.

This is the topic for the next chapter.

Chapter 6

THE DYNAMICS OF THE MOURNER'S FEELINGS

As we begin to discern the diverse feelings the mourner is experiencing and recognize the emotional journey he is traversing, we may be able to see an emerging pattern that is natural and appropriate for his situation. We will see that these feelings arise from an identifiable need, and carry the mourner toward a recognizable goal.

It is essential for the bereavement counselor to be convinced that healthy progress through grief *requires* passage through these emotions. The sequence, intensity, and duration of these feelings always vary from individual to individual. They are always affected by the lifelong culture, coping mechanisms, and personality patterns of individual mourners, as well as by the particular circumstances of the beloved's death. Yet, the overall general pattern of normal healthy adjustment to grief can be perceived, described, and dynamically understood.

The grief process has a sensible and comprehensible dynamic. There are necessary and natural factors that determine the process of healthy passage through the trauma of loss. The bereavement counselor should employ both his empathy and his intelligence to understand this dynamic, and to reckon with it throughout the counseling process.

This dynamic can be formulated through three general concepts:

1. Each of the mourner's feelings can be grouped into one of two categories, fundamental or peripheral.

2. Usually, the peripheral feelings arise in the earlier stages of the bereavement journey. They function as a protective mechanism, aiming to help the mourner to delay, avoid, or altogether escape the pain of encountering the fundamental emotions. Sooner or later the mourner will move to the realization, at some level of perception, that this is an unachievable goal.

3. Healthy completion of the healing process is possible when the mourner acknowledges and lives with his feelings, of either or both categories, and allows himself an opportunity to confront and wrestle with them.

The goal of the bereavement counselor is to introduce the bereaved person to this process in a friendly and caring way, with empathy, understanding, and support. Through the counseling process we wish to assure him that, once he has tasted this experience in our company and with our support, he will be in a stronger position to continue the journey, even without us.

The eight sessions of pastoral bereavement counseling are not intended to be, nor should they be promoted as the complete journey of healing. The goal is, as we have said earlier, to support the mourner in taking the first steps, i.e., in helping him towards authentic engagement with a sad reality, but also with genuine hope that he will ultimately experience a measure of true healing.

THE TWO CATEGORIES

The primal, fundamental, core feelings of bereavement are: fear, helplessness, anger, and guilt.

The peripheral feelings arise from the mechanisms that facilitate a gradual circuitous exposure to, instead of a rapid immersion into, the traumatic fundamental torments. The mourner experiences them as shock, disorientation, mental confusion, avoidance of normal activity, frenzied scurrying about, denial, daydreaming, and illusory perception.

Whichever feelings the mourner expresses during the counseling sessions—be they of the primal trauma or of the peripheral shield—they will need to be accurately understood and categorized by the counselor, in order that he may correctly visualize that portion of the mourner's journey that he is accompanying.

His identification and categorization of the mourner's feelings will enable him to assess correctly the position that his 2-month participation occupies within the continuum of the mourner's journey from grief to healing.

The counselor is most effective when he recognizes *both* the limited extent of his role in the healing process, *and at the same time* the significant influence that that limited portion can have on the complete journey.

Since Pastoral Bereavement Counselors are engaged with their clients during a 2-month period within a year of their bereavement, they will usually touch emotions of both categories. When the emotions that emerge during the counseling are correctly recognized, when those emotions are handled therapeutically during that 2-month period, and when an expectation of continuing progress and further journeying is transmitted to the mourner during those 2 months, the counselor will have greatly enhanced the probability of genuine healing.

This is a manageable and achievable goal.

The design of Pastoral Bereavement Counseling recognizes the magnitude of the task of effectively helping the bereaved. We believe that the system we are advocating can extend the influence of a few hours' effort to significantly affect a lifetime.

What is crucial in achieving this goal is not which emotions are reached during the 2 months—whether primal or peripheral—but the therapeutic skill with which these emotions are handled in the counselor-mourner relationship. And it is crucial for the development and perfection of those skills to appreciate why it is natural and legitimate for these emotions to arise in the aftermath of a loss.

THE DYNAMICS OF THE PRIMAL EMOTIONS

It is natural, it is to be expected, and it seems rather obvious when we allow ourselves to empathize, that the mourners should have intense fears—fears of a drastic change in their lives, fears of being unable to competently face the future, fears of loneliness, fears of the risks in attempting new relationships, fears of never being loved again, fearing their own dying and fearing the death of other loved ones, fear of fate turning against them, fear of God continuing to punish them, fear of getting old, of being abandoned, of dying as painfully as their beloved one—or, more painfully than their beloved one, fear of the burial process, fear of being punished in hell, fear of their lives being judged meaningless, fear of no longer enjoying the pleasures of life.

Such fears are natural, they are to be expected, as are all the additional nuances and particular dreads that each one of us has carried as part of our lifelong cultural and psychological baggage.

All the possible formulations of the fears that arise in the mourning heart could never be completely listed, nor does the bereavement counselor need to compile a full compendium of human fears. But a bereavement counselor *does* need to recognize and reckon with the relentless torment fueled by the elemental fears of the human heart in its confrontation with existential sorrow.

No wonder our ancestors conjured up the vision of an Angel of Death and the mythic figure of The Grim Reaper. Modern western culture has no comparable myth or vision that encapsulates the demonic force that malevolently inflicts upon us pain and fear and helplessness. At the early stages of confrontation with loss the mourner is caught in a vortex of fears that he can only dimly identify, and of which he is totally terrified.

In preparation for his task of seeking to help the mourner, the Pastoral Bereavement Counselor should attempt to incorporate into his imagination, as empathically and sincerely as possible, the depth and force of the mourner's elemental fears. They are natural and legitimate and dynamically comprehensible. Bereavement counseling strategy should in no way deny, or avoid, or seek to minimize the power and legitimacy of the mourner's fears.

Neither should our strategy overlook the sense of helplessness in the face of death—which can move toward hopelessness and despair—that is also natural and legitimate and dynamically understandable. Death is the irrefutable challenge to the delusion that we are in control of our own destinies.

When we lose someone who was near and close and part of our lives, we are jarred out of our comfortable illusion that we can plan and manage our lives. Suddenly, our vaunted power is ashes and air. Suddenly, life and love are taken out of our hands. In a flash our castles of happiness crash to the ground, and the firm footing under our steps becomes a gaping abyss.

Suddenly, the future which we took for granted is fickle and uncertain, and the solid glitter of life is no more. We are not the captain of our ship, we're not even crew members. We are dispensable and insignificant. A bereaved person can never return to a sense of absolute security.

There can be no quick bedrock acceptance of the pervasive sense of helplessness forced upon us by death. Religion, philosophy, poetry, and folk wisdom can cushion the blow, but they are misused when they are applied as a substitute for "working through" the elemental feelings.* The counselor who wishes to help the mourner journey through bereavement must recognize the radical alterations in thinking about life and love and an insecure future, that death has brought into his client's consciousness. He should prepare himself to accept such feelings—

---

*Indeed, basic religious philosophy insists upon a serious view of man's duties to God precisely because God, not man, is the master of man's destiny. But this is not a conclusion at which one can arrive easily or automatically. It requires contemplation, prayerful consideration, debating, wondering about, "wrestling with" and "working through," even for the man or woman of faith. In a sense therefore, "working through" and accepting God as the Master of our destinies in the aftermath of a bereavement is in itself a significant *religious* activity.

if the client expresses them—as legitimate and normal, as non-dismissible and not to be philosophized away.

At some point during the eight sessions, the mourner can also be expected to express feelings of anger, directly or indirectly. Many people have difficulty talking about their anger, some for psychocultural reasons, some out of religious fear of offending God. But it is the counselor's task to allow expression of anger, to encourage it if it begins timidly, and to convey his conviction that it is healthy and permissible.

The counselor should regard expressions of anger as temporary, in most cases, but as very necessary for the mourner to ventilate. It is a normal and healthy emotional stage that all mourners have to pass through. It is an essential part of the dynamics of response to a significant loss.

How could we expect it to be otherwise? Anger is a normal and healthy reaction when we feel robbed and wronged. The mourner is that human being who is contemplating the painful fact that someone who was precious and beloved and a light in his life, has been taken beyond his reach. He can no longer have what he wants, he is angry because he feels cheated. He needs an opportunity to release that anger. It is well known that suppressed rage is a prime cause of clinical depression.

The Pastoral Bereavement Counselor understands that anger is a valid, justifiable, and healthy emotion that a mourner may feel and, if he wishes, may express. He will further come to understand that the mourner's anger will often be general and unspecific. Often, when it emerges, it may not be directed against anyone or against anything in particular. In essence, the mourner is angry because he finds himself in a tragic and impossible situation.

He is angry because he feels cheated, because he feels lost and alone, because he is beset by fears, and because he senses his loss of control. He feels the world's cards stacked against him, that fate/God is cursing him.

He is angry at the inner turmoil of fears and rudderlessness raging within him. He feels doubly assaulted—by the environment operating against his wishes, and by his inner torments and perplexities. He feels spiritual and psychological pressures from many directions, which threaten to push him further out of control.

It is therefore natural for him to want to explode, to cast off the restraints of politeness, to want to shake his fist at God or at Whoever is out there, to curse, to hurt himself and others, to act crazily or irrationally. A mourner's anger, although a demonstration of desperation, is essentially normal, understandable, and legitimate. It may be frightening, but it is not unhealthy.

Many mourners whom we have counseled had difficulty understanding that general and unspecific anger is still genuine anger, just as real as when it is vented on a specific target. They experienced psychological confusion when they felt blocked by cultural or religious constraints from directing their anger at a specific entity.

Often the mourner will say, "Yes, I'm angry, but I don't know if it's right! How can I be angry at the doctor, he tried his best! How can I be angry at God, it's a sin! Sometimes I'm terribly angry at my wife for dying and leaving me, what's wrong with me?! I'm angry and confused and upset, I don't understand, and I don't know how to deal with my feelings. And that makes me even angrier!"

A counselor's response in such a situation would be eminently different than that of a friend or well-meaning companion. The therapeutic response would be rooted in the realization that the mourner is struggling for a logical answer to what in reality is a nonlogical problem. What is needed is not, "There's no reason to be angry." Such a response is a futile attempt to direct the mourner to be reasonable at a time when, due to circumstances beyond his control, he *cannot* be.

What the mourner needs is to know that the counselor recognizes the actuality of his anger. What the mourner needs is to hear through the counselor's words, and to sense through the counselor's attitude, a *validation* of the legitimacy of his anger. Depending upon whether this expression of anger was the first in the sessions or whether there had been previous ones, the therapeutic response could range from:

1. patient silence (simple acceptance); to

2. "You seem to be feeling very angry, and I want you to know I think it's okay" (labeling and legitimization); to

3. "You seem to be feeling a great deal of anger, and it's making you feel very uncomfortable" (reflection); to

4. "It may be that you'll continue to be angry at your situation for some time. I think it's okay to feel that way, and I don't want you to run away from it even though it's painful. Try to recognize that you're really very angry. It's okay to be aware of it. What I want you to do is to stay with this anger, to let yourself feel it, as much as you can. Let's see what happens, it may be that it's part of a process" ("staying with" and "working through").

We cite these possible responses at this point only to illustrate how understanding the theoretical dynamics of the bereavement process points to effective counseling technique. A fuller treatment of recommended counseling techniques will be given in the next chapter.

Of course, in addition to understanding the theory of the process and applying the skills correctly, we hope that the Pastoral Bereavement Counselor will be motivated by empathy for another's pain, and by his desire to heal and bless a suffering child of God.

The Fourth Primal Emotion

The fourth fundamental feeling is guilt. The anger at being forced to suffer pain is so intense and continuous that it is turned inward. The hurt and disappointment that has been feeding upon itself, still looking for a specific target, becomes directed against oneself.

For no apparent rational reason the mourner begins to blame himself for real or imagined imperfections, and seems to find an irrational satisfaction in condemning himself. We have already cited a number of examples of a mourner's typical protestations of guilt.

This emotion usually figures so prominently and obsessively in the mourner's feelings, and is so universally encountered in the normal bereavement process, that it deserves to be regarded as a central element in the trauma of bereavement.

The dynamic of the griever's guilt seems to arise from a deeper source than the other primal feelings. A straightforward explanation, as was used in describing the process that produces fear, helplessness, and anger, will not suffice to explain the irrationality and compulsiveness with which guilt is connected in the mourner's situation. The counselor will notice that as soon as the mourner allows himself to tap into his deep feelings, and if the requisite therapeutic rapport has been established, there will *always* come forth a sense of guilt.

Whatever imperfections may have existed in the relationship between the deceased and the survivor are exacerbated, in the mourner's perception, into sins and crimes. Words, deeds, decisions that were uttered or implemented during the weeks before the death are often seized upon by the mourner for relentless review and compulsive reiteration. Through expressions of insistent breast-beating and self-flagellation, the mourner seems to be driven by an irrational and insatiable desire to punish himself.

The counselor may try to place the normal mistakes or misjudgments that are common in human behavior into a rational context. He may suggest that the mourner need not feel guilty since he could not have known—no one could have known—what the outcome of necessary decisions would be. More often than not, the mourner will resist such appeals to reason.

The counselor may hear the mourner saying such things as, "No, I should have known, it was my fault. If I had called the doctor sooner" (or, "if I had insisted upon an ambulance right away," etc.) "I would have saved him, Max would be alive today."

I have come to understand that the rationale for the mourner's guilt lies not in the action or inaction, the wisdom or stupidity of a particular decision, but rather in the nature of the bereavement situation itself. It does not arise from particular circumstances, but from the universal factors that are operating in a *healthy* reaction to a devastating loss.

In fact, there may be two separate sources from which the mourner's guilt arises, and both often create feelings of discomfort that resonate with and reinforce each other.

One of the sources of mourner's guilt is the ambivalence inherent in recognizing oneself as a survivor. A mourner experiences, at the core of his being, a conflict between limitless love and extreme selfishness. On the one hand, there is a genuine sadness at the cutoff of the life of the beloved; on the other, there is a surprising covert exultation at being alive.

We call it survivor's guilt, but it is a complex and convoluted emotion. The mourner feels a double unease—guilt at being the survivor of the love union ("It should have been me, not her, I didn't love her enough"), and a marring of his joy of survival because it is incomplete without her.

All these feelings are genuinely valid, the sadness and gladness are equally authentic and equally legitimate; yet they are in paradoxical conflict. They enter the mourner's awareness at the same time, and they remain side by side for a long time. Guilt arises in the mourner's heart, necessarily and unavoidably, as a product of the deeply imbedded and existential antimony between sadness and happiness that lies at the very center of the grief experience.

The mourner is only dimly aware of this built-in paradox in the emotional reactions to grief. He is confused and unable to identify these troublesome feelings. Even if it were explained to him and satisfied his intellect, he would be emotionally unable to integrate the inherent and unavoidable paradox. Therefore he wallows in a vague uneasiness; he perceives a dim discontent within his emotions which is intensified by its indistinctness and mystery. It is this feeling that he expresses as guilt.

The Pastoral Bereavement Counselor who wishes to heal a mourner's wounds must seek to gain a clear understanding of the nature and dynamics of guilt. He must adopt a counseling stance that will reckon with the irrationality, vagueness, and complexity of this emotion that the mourner feels as guilt. He will not succeed if he responds with a logical directive that "There's no reason to feel guilty."

This is why our Commission recommends that clergy and others who wish to become adept at bereavement counseling undertake supplementary training. They will need to unlearn the methods that are based on logic, and substitute an approach that seeks to guide a mourner through an irrational maze of vagueness and a complex paradox. The techniques that we recommend and will list in the next chapter are selected for that purpose.

A second source of the psychological and emotional factors that produce a sense of guilt in bereavement is the mourner's unconscious need to reassert a sense of control over his own destiny. This too leads to conflicting feelings. One part of his being perceives that he is forced to accept the reality of loss of control while another part is squirming and rebelling against it. This is a second ambivalence that is troublesome for the mourner's feelings, although perhaps not as sharp as the sadness-gladness conflict.

As we have discussed earlier in this chapter, the death of a loved one is the greatest challenge to one's sense of being the master of one's own fate. Our illusion of control is shattered on the brute fact of irretrievable separation. After an initial period of numbness, shock, and disbelief, the mourner has to proceed to grapple with the challenge to his sense of control.

Slowly, he begins to hope that there yet remains some area where his will counts, where he will be able to reestablish a feeling of limited mastery over his environment. In the process he searches for some excuse, some answer as to why his previous exercise of will failed to prevent his beloved's death.

The path toward this desired rehabilitation of his sense of mastery leads him through the feelings of anger, blame, and guilt. If he sinned and was punished by losing his beloved, he unreasonably but compulsively hopes that by feeling guilty, blaming and punishing himself, he will expiate his wrongdoing and reinherit control over his life.

It is important that the bereavement counselor understands the sources of the fundamental feelings of grief, and the dynamic that invests these feelings with their compulsive and irrational characteristics. But this analysis is not meant to be imparted to the counselee-mourner. Pastoral Bereavement

Counseling is designed to be exclusively supportive, never analytic. Explaining to the mourner the reasons for the way he feels serves no therapeutic purpose.

The counselor should not cast himself into the role of lecturer, psychiatrist, or wisdom-dispenser. That could interfere with the formation of the optimum counselor-mourner relationship, where the mourner sees the counselor as warm, friendly, trustworthy, concerned, open to listening and sharing in the mourner's suffering. The principal task of the bereavement counselor—from the mourner's point of view—is to be neither an adviser nor an explainer. It is to be a listener and a companion-in-feeling.

THE DYNAMICS OF THE PERIPHERAL EMOTIONS

The dynamics of the group of peripheral emotions are more easily and simply explained than the fundamental ones. They are of two kinds—a mechanism of delay, and a mechanism of denial. Nature has put both mechanisms into operation in our psychological system as a protection against too rapid immersion into the full pain and torment of grief. They are God's ways of being merciful.

Delay and denial both serve to cushion the harsh and cruel blow that death delivers. They soften the starkness of loss and provide an opportunity for the mourner to slowly get accustomed to sadness and pain. Delay and denial are two psychological devices that permit a tentative, hesitant approach to a frightening experience.

The mechanisms of delay can be understood as arising from the consequences of shock. The traumatic reality of the loss is so overwhelming that the body's processes are shocked and disrupted out of their normal pattern. This is an instinctive and involuntary process. The mourner is not aware of them, and will usually not report about them explicitly. Instead, mourners will report on a behavior change that frightens them. They wonder when and if they will be able to return to their customary habits.

The shock has produced strange feelings and unusual behavior, sometimes so bizarre and prolonged that the mourner begins to be concerned about his future functioning. Often, this is what has brought them to request bereavement counseling. Examples of these behavioral changes were described in the previous chapter.

The mourner may report episodes of emotional deadening, a lethargy of feeling, a numbness of body and spirit—which may be the result of the psychological shock or a phase of depression, or a little of both. He may also express concern about absent-mindedness, forgetfulness, disorientation, mental confusion, or uncharacteristic rudeness. These may also be the consequences of the initial shock to the system.

Unless these behaviors persist throughout the weeks of the counseling, the counselor may regard them as temporary manifestations of the grieving process.

Nature's second shield against too sudden confrontation with pain is the mechanism of denial. Some of the normal manifestations of this natural mechanism are conscious avoidance, withdrawal from regular routine, or its opposite—frenzied activity—compulsive attention to detail, episodic daydreaming, procrastination, and hallucinatory illusions.

The bereavement counselor understands that these mechanisms, although disruptive and bizarre to the mourner, are natural and healthy, and accepts them as an appropriate portion of the mourner's journey. He seeks to help the mourner by projecting this attitude of acceptance and assurance of basic normalcy. Part of his task is to remain alert to any obstruction in the flow of emotional process.

The counselor does not try to hasten the mourner's journey. He should not, in his own mind, chart a schedule for the weeks ahead as to when the mourner might come to experience a particular feeling. He should let the mourner move along at his own pace—along the way, supporting, monitoring, and empathizing.

In these last two chapters we have described the mourner's feelings as we have experienced them in our structured counseling sessions. We have put forth the reasons and dynamic explanations for these emotions, and have made suggestions about the counselor's basic orientation as he goes about his task.

In the next chapter, we will outline the applicable counseling techniques that the Commision recommends to help in healing the mourner's wounds.

Chapter 7

A THERAPEUTIC RESPONSE TO THE MOURNER'S DISTRESS

The counseling techniques that we will describe in this chapter are based upon the pioneering work of Carl Rogers, the founder of client-centered therapy. We believe that his approach is especially suited for bereavement counseling because its theoretical formulation of what a counselor should aim for in general precisely parallels the mourner's needs in particular.

Client-centered therapy hypothesizes that emotional health and optimum personality development are enhanced when the counselor treats the counselee's feelings with great care and high regard. This is more than just a device for establishing friendly rapport. It is the essence and foundation for wholesome personality development insofar as it can be affected by the counseling transaction.

According to Rogerian theory, the therapeutic purpose is best carried forward when the client is guided to a recognition of his deep feelings and to an appreciation that honest awareness is the path to emotional health.

This approach is especially appropriate for use in bereavement counseling. As we have seen, the mourner's principal need, especially in his initial reaching out, is for recognition of and skilled attention to the emotional churning he is experiencing. He needs someone willing and able to offer him honest empathy. He needs a counselor to carry through a contract of sustained empathy and skillful support during at least a portion of his emotional journey. This is what the Pastoral Bereavement Counselor aims to be, and for which the Rogerian approach provides the most relevant and useful counseling tools.

During our counseling sessions we aim to:

1. encourage recognition of feelings;
2. legitimize awareness of feelings;
3. explore the depth of the mourner's feelings;
4. help the mourner to appreciate the importance of being aware of his deep feelings;
5. aid the mourner in "staying with" and "working through" his feelings;
6. recognize movement and progress;
7. commend movement and progress;
8. portray change and movement through the emotions of grief as a process and a journey;
9. implant hope that, by continuing to be aware of and "work through" his feelings, the mourner will, in time, be able to complete the journey.

How do we accomplish this? How do we move the mourner along the path of these attitudinal changes? What are the specific techniques that the counselor should employ to reach these aims?

THE TEN RECOMMENDED COUNSELING SKILLS:

We suggest the following 10 techniques. We recommend them on the basis of our successful experiences in this field over the past 12 years.

1. Listening
2. Reflection
3. Identifying and labeling
4. Assurance of initial and sustained support
5. Assurance of normalcy

6. "Staying with"
7. "Working through"
8. Noting and commending every sign of progress
9. Use of words and ideas—religious philosophy, wisdom, poetry
10. Terminating—therapeutic conclusion

1. Listening

This is an art that we may take too much for granted. Some aspiring Pastoral Bereavement Counselors—especially a pulpit clergyperson—may need to give some time to practicing listening, because it may call for a radical change in the habit of relating to others.

The listening technique has two dimensions, one negative, and one positive. There is one, a self-restraint—don't talk, keep silent—and second, a straining to clearly understand, a positive effort *to hear the words and their meaning.*

Listening, if we seek to practice the art proficiently, is best thought of as active empathy. It is not passive, it is much more than an absence of talk. It is an intensive involvement with the client's emotional state. It is really a nonverbal way of saying, "I care for you and what is going on inside of you." It is giving attention and sending out signals of alertness and of antenna-raising. It means earnest listening, loving eye contact, silent absorption of the mourner's troubles.

The art of listening can be experimented with even in an unstructured relationship. Try it the next time an ordinary conversation begins to move into an area of emotional concern.

Instead of giving advice (even if it's expert advice), which really means that you're responding more to *your* needs—(e.g., you want to avoid the subject, or, you feel the need to control the other, or, you want to feel important/wise, or, you need to have the other dependent on you), listen and remain silent as long as possible.

At some point your friend will notice the change in your behavior. He will begin to perceive that you are now willing to *listen* to him, perhaps for the first time, and that you're really caring about *his* needs above your own.

Your silence doesn't provide the solution or cure to the

problem, but it telegraphs your genuine willingness to share the other's emotional concerns. In the case of a bereaved friend, or client, that message can be crucial.

2. Reflection

This is a counseling skill that should be employed only in a counseling relationship. It is inappropriate in a friendship relationship.

Reflection is an intervention by the counselor to aid the client in recognizing and clarifying his bedrock feelings. It is a gentle step towards uncovering dimly felt fears that the client tends to avoid because he senses them as potentially troublesome and painful.

It is an intervention that needs to be applied firmly but with empathy. The counselor attempts to guide the mourner towards a more perceptive insight about his deep feelings. By this intervention, the counselor can function as the mirror that reflects back to the mourner a truer vision of his emotional state.

When skillfully applied, reflection is an educational and supportive process whose source is largely unrecognized by the mourner. Ideally, the mourner perceives the new insight as arising from his own wrestling with his grief. It is valuable and effective because it can alert the mourner to a fundamental insight in a relatively short period of time and in a manner that does not make him feel overly dependent on the counselor.

In a sense, journeying toward a truer understanding of the feelings of grief is a natural process that every mourner would move to, if he allowed himself sufficient time to reflect upon his loss and to contemplate his new reality. But because death is such a frightful happening, and because profound contemplation is a lost art in our times, most mourners never make a sustained effort to confront their pain.

Structured bereavement counseling provides an effective setting for this necessary activity. The counselor's use of reflection as a therapeutic technique initiates the mourner into the process of facing his deep feelings and beginning his journey through them.

"I don't understand why this happened. Henry was such a good man. He never refused a plea for charity. We raised our children properly and tried to be decent human beings. He and I had so much to look forward to—now suddenly, this blow—two hours in the hospital and Henry's gone. It's all so meaningless! Why? Why?"

"I think I'm hearing a feeling behind these questions."

"I can't understand it, it doesn't make sense. We deserved a future together. Maybe I didn't deserve it,* but Henry certainly did. I wish someone could explain it to me, then maybe I'd have some peace. Can you explain it to me?"

"It would be more useful if I could point you toward something else, toward your feelings inside. When you're saying these words, what feelings are you experiencing? What's going on inside your heart and stomach?"

"I'm nervous and agitated, I don't feel good, my stomach is all tied up in knots—I'm very upset—I don't know what I'm feeling."

"Well, I guess what you're feeling is a protest, a kind of rebellion. You don't like what's happening to you, and you're angry at what's going on."

"Yes, I'm certainly angry—about me and about what's happened to Henry—yes, I think I'm angry—as a matter of fact, I think I'm very angry!"

As the session proceeded, the counselor allowed the flow of anger to come out. He encouraged expressions of feeling, on any subject, and pointed out any signs of protest or anger, whether directed at the world in general or someone in particular. He allowed and legitimized any and all such expressions—by respectful attentiveness, by empathic silence, by a nod of the head, by open rejoinders of assent, by short phrases of agreement. "I understand, it's okay, go on, tell me more, I'm interested."

The counselor tried to convey to the mourner his basic conviction that a bereaved person is permitted to feel anger and to protest his fate. Both counselor and mourner began to join in the recognition that there is raw primal emotion underneath the genteel search for meaning, and that in fact this is imbedded in the nature of the situation.

---

*A hint of the feeling of guilt, but the counselor chooses not to pick up on it at this time.

At one point the counselor said, "You will not be able to pass through the state of anger until you cease disguising your feelings. You have to stop masking them behind politeness. The sooner you recognize your bedrock feelings of anger, the sooner anger will lose its power in your life."

Over the next few sessions the mourner was brought to recognize that anger "in general" or "in particular" is neither unnatural or unhealthy. For himself, the counselor noted that a griever's apparent search for meaning has both a philosophical and emotional dimension, the former being largely overt, the latter usually covert and hidden. The counselor became clearer in his own understanding that both aspects need to be recognized and engaged.

The clergyperson as theologian and preacher is in a position to answer the philosophical questions. The clergyperson in the role of counselor should aim primarily to deal with the mourner's emotional needs.

Let me cite a second example of reflection. A retired doctor whose wife had died after a three-month bout with cancer was expressing sorrow and loneliness and fear.

"Steve, what were your feelings this week?"

"I'm very uncomfortable coming home to an empty house. I miss her very much. I don't sleep well at night. I keep waking up through the night, thinking about her. We had forty years together, through thick and thin, many times she was my right hand."

"Is this what you think about at night?"

"Not only at night, sometimes during the day, too. I remember how good she was for me, and sometimes I think I wasn't nice enough to her. Me, I'm supposed to be the big doctor, I give everybody advice, but I couldn't cure my own wife—I don't know—maybe I didn't act fast enough—I should have noticed the early symptoms—and then it was too late—I keep thinking that I failed her—"

"Are you blaming yourself? Do you feel guilty?"

"Maybe—(pause, counselor remaining silent)—but I don't have reason to—nobody would have thought of the worst—we thought it was an eye problem, that it could be fixed by new glasses—we decided to go for a week's vacation—now I'm thinking we should have gone directly to the hospital—maybe we would have caught it in time."

"This question, this doubt in your mind, half blaming yourself, half justifying yourself, it's a conflict inside of you, correct?"

"Yes, I feel myself struggling with it, going back and forth in my mind. Should I really feel guilty? Is this what's bothering me at night? . . . and during the day?"

"It might be, I'm not sure. But whatever your feeling is, I'd like you to focus on it and try to be clear about it."

(A few seconds of silence)

"Why?"

"That's not so important now. What's more important now is to let yourself feel—whatever it is that you're feeling—if it's guilt—if it's blame—whatever it is—and to recognize it."

"Come to think of it, I do feel guilty. I didn't do enough. Why should she be dead, and I'm still living? She was a better wife to me than I was a husband to her. It's not fair, life doesn't make sense."

"I think you're recognizing some guilt and some anger, both feelings may be in you."

"I think you're right, I think maybe that's what I'm feeling—I think I've done something wrong—I'm angry at myself and I'm also angry at others. Why am I feeling this way? Am I right or wrong? Should I try to change myself?"

"Right now, that's not what I'm suggesting. Let's take it step by step. Right now I want you to recognize those two feelings—anger and guilt—that are giving you a lot of trouble. Try to focus on those feelings and say to yourself, 'Maybe he's right, maybe that's what I'm going through, anger at everyone and anger at myself.' And, let's try to talk about this some more, next week."

Reflection is a key technique in the process of structured bereavement counseling. It enhances the mourner's health in five dynamic ways.

1. It *clarifies* the mourner's feelings, which are usually confused, vague, and ambivalent. It suggests a formulation that,

even if it is only partially correct, reduces the mourner's confusion. We will discuss this in greater detail in the section on identifying and labeling.

2. It *legitimizes* the mourner's feelings, whatever they are. It is the counselor's way of declaring, in a therapeutic manner, that the emotions of grief are worthy and significant—not only to the mourner, but to the one who has undertaken to help him. It says to the mourner, "Your feelings are important enough to be examined and contemplated and dwelt upon, they are not to be disregarded."

3. It is *a powerful demonstration of empathy*. Its unspoken message from the counselor is, "I care enough about your pain to do more than hear it. I'm ready to absorb it and to feel it and to think about it. See, I have assimilated it sufficiently into my consciousness and intellect to the point where I can formulate it precisely enough to present it to *your* intellect and consciousness. It is proof that I care deeply for your health and welfare, and have invested a portion of *my* thought and experience on your behalf."

4. *It is nonjudgmental*. It allows the mourner to remain comfortable with his emotions, and does not raise his defenses against revealing intimate thoughts. It accepts all emotions as equally worthy and valid. It conveys the counselor's therapeutic posture toward the mourner—"Feel free to speak about anything you wish. Even your deepest thoughts are okay to express. There are no emotions for which you will be condemned or of which you need to feel ashamed. I wish to encourage you to speak freely about your pain and sadness or whatever is bothering you. Whatever you tell me will be incorporated into my emotional experiences, as will be demonstrated by my mirroring back to you your own feelings."

5. *It conditions the mourner towards self-reliance* and nondependence on the counselor. It helps to define the counselor's image as the mourner should see him—as a helper and guide, as a supporter through the bereavement process—not as an oracle or wisdom-dispenser or automatic healer.

The counselor's use of reflection conveys to the counselee the understanding that it is up to *him*, the *mourner*, to do his own grief-work. The counselor's role is to initiate, to guide, to facilitate the process—not to provide ready-made answers.

Pastoral Bereavement Counseling has a limited number of sessions, and the counselor's presence in the mourner's life is only temporary. For the long pull, the mourner will have no one to rely upon but himself. The process of teaching him to rely upon his own self-awareness—which the mourner will need for the long pull—is well begun by early and frequent use of reflection.

3. Identifying and Labeling

This is a half-step beyond reflection. We recommend that the counselor repeat and reiterate the mourner's recognition of his deep emotions after they have been brought to the mourner's consciousness through reflection. We use every opportunity to emphasize and repeat the name of the feeling that the mourner is describing. This reinforces and concretizes the conscious perception of the feeling that was stimulated by the counselor to emerge from a dim vagueness to a new clarity.

It prepares the mourner for the intensification of the emotional experiencing that is required in the later process of "staying with" and "working through."

Let me cite an illustration from our case histories. In the second session with a widow of 5 months, she began to speak of her near-hallucinatory images.

"What's the matter with me? Am I going crazy? I begin to make myself a little supper, and at six o'clock I hear his key turning in the door. I look at the door and I half expect to see him opening it. Once, I called out, 'Bill, wait a minute, I'm coming.' How long is this going to go on? Am I acting strangely?"

"Try to remember. How were you feeling when you thought you heard his key in the door?"

"Very sorry for myself, very lonely, missing him very much, wishing he would really come in."

"Exactly, and maybe the wish became the father to the vision—so, what were you doing—what would you call it?"

"Letting my imagination go wild, just giving in to my wishes, wishful thinking. That's not so good, is it?"

"It's not so bad—but what is it that you were doing, in wishing that he were home, and then you heard his key in the door?"

"I think you'd call it wishing it were true—fantasizing."

"Yes, that's right, that's what I'd call it—daydreaming—your powers of imagination were so intense, because you miss him so and need him so, that you actually dreamed it with your eyes open—you were daydreaming."

"Is there something wrong with that?"

"No, at this stage in your situation I don't think there's anything wrong with that. But I want you to know what it is that seems to be happening. You were daydreaming."

At the next session she told of another episode—gazing out the window and watching people come from behind the building and turning the corner in her direction.

"I was daydreaming again. I kept watching the people in the street from my window, and found myself commanding Bill to be the next one—'C'mon Bill, you be the next one.' What did you call it? . . . wishing? . . . fantasizing?"

"Daydreaming."

"Yes, that's what I've been doing for some time now, only I didn't realize it. It was so strange that I put it out of my mind. I didn't want to admit it to myself.

"Yes, that's what I think it is—daydreaming."

She went on to report an episode of imagining Bill in the bed and reaching out and talking to him. She went on to say, "That's daydreaming, isn't it? Half of me facing reality and half of me denying it."

I silently realized that I wouldn't be able to improve on that description or that labeling.

During the next session, there was no mention of any illusory phenomenon, nor in the session after that. Near the end of that session I wondered about that absence and wanted to make sure. I asked, "Any episodes of imagination?"

"You mean daydreaming, don't you. No, I don't have such thoughts anymore. I'm more realistic, I don't have to fight the truth. Every time I began to daydream and realized what it was I was doing, the image went away. Is that progress?"

"I'd rather not call it that. I'd rather call it passing through a certain stage of the mourning process. Tell me, how do you feel about not daydreaming about Bill anymore?"

"To tell the truth, I'm a little sad to give it up. It was somehow comforting to picture him in my imagination. But when you gave it a name and told me what it was—daydreaming—it kind of helped me to wean myself away from it. I think you're right, I think I have passed through a stage."

Let me cite a second illustration of the role played by *identifying and labeling* in counseling the bereaved. Elizabeth had been mourning her husband's death for 6 months when she first came to our Pastoral Bereavement Counseling program.

Interestingly, she usually began each session with a whistling-in-the-dark pattern—"I'm really getting better, I think I'm all right, people tell me that I look good and that it's good that I'm cheerful and that they're proud of me. It'll take just a little while longer and I'm sure I'll be completely fine."

The counselor allowed her to move on that way, and usually in less than 10 minutes, she moved to expressions of lesser certainty about her progress and her future—"But only one thing is still bothering me—as soon as I get over that, I'll be fine." She would then go on to a litany of symptoms that seemed to the counselor to indicate more cover-up than facing reality.

During the first four sessions she spoke about her terrible loneliness, her jealousy of other people living and loving normally, her frenzied activity on and off her job, her volunteering for overtime because she desperately needed to keep busy to keep her mind off her loss, her walking the streets blindly, her aimless mixing with crowds and noise at a neighboring shopping mall. She said she wanted to get better, but her frenzied activity, her sadness, and pervasive depression appeared to the counselor to be symptoms of a repressed anger that she was unable to acknowledge.

During the fifth session the counselor began to reflect back her anger. The exchange quickly progressed from hesitant use of the word to definite labeling.

"But I don't want to feel angry . . . I'm supposed to accept this . . . I'll get over it in time."

"I'm wondering whether there's any connection between what you just said, and your keeping yourself so busy that you won't have time to think."

"What do you mean?"

"Well, you said that maybe you *are* angry but that you don't *want* to feel angry."

"You mean, that's a contradiction."

"It's a conflict on an emotional level. You're being pulled inside by two opposite feelings—you're angry but you don't *want to* be angry—that's what I heard you saying. You were saying it to me, but maybe you are also recognizing your own deep feelings."

"What good would it do for me to feel angry?"

"What good does it do to deny your anger?"

There was a long pause.

"So you want me to be angry!"

"No, I want you to let yourself be angry if you feel it inside yourself. I don't want you to make yourself be angry, to force it. I want you to let yourself feel it if it comes up naturally."

"You mean that I've been stopping myself from a natural feeling?"

"Maybe."

"Is this what's causing some of the other things?—the rushing around?—the terrible loneliness?—I just realized that I'm angry at being lonely. It's not only that I don't like it, I'm angry against it. I hate the world, I hate myself, I hate God, I hate life. I'm boxed into this situation and I don't like it. I'm all by myself and there's no way out. You're right, I *am* angry!"

"I think you're really angry, and you've got to let it come out."

"How?"

"By admitting to yourself—yes, I'm angry. I want to protest about it, I want to shake my fist at someone."

"But I can't do that."

"But you can recognize your inside feeling! And you can talk to me about it, and look forward to telling me about it next week."

"I can't say it to anyone I know, they'll think I'm losing control. I'll lose my friends, I don't want to be rude."

"Why don't you try writing it down. Take a blank piece of paper and write down whatever comes to your mind. Don't worry about grammar or structure, just pour out whatever you're feeling. If you want to, bring it to our session next week, if you'd like me to see it."

The next session began with a 5-minute outburst, a difference from her usual pattern of self-assurance.

"Boy, was I angry all last week, since our last meeting. I really did what you suggested, I allowed myself to be angry. I was so angry that I looked for people upon whom to vent my fury. I yelled at the delivery boy, I yelled at the sales clerk. I had a chip on my shoulder all week. I kind of welcomed a chance to meet people who I could find an excuse to lash out against.

"I think maybe I'm a little better, but boy, did I express anger all last week! I wasn't even sorry for the people I was yelling at—I not only allowed myself to yell at them, I was actually looking forward to doing it. Is that too much? Did I go too far?"

"From what you're telling me, I would guess that you were aware of what you were doing and how you felt inside."

"Very much aware. The anger is still in me. Maybe it's a little better, but I'm still angry."

"Did you put any of your feelings on paper? Did you write about it?"

"Yes, I have it here to show to you. There's something else I found to do in the past week that maybe helped me to release some more anger. I got up each morning at 5:30 A.M. and I followed the exercise class on television. Some of the exercises are hard to do, but I reminded myself that I'm angry at the world and I took it out on the push-ups and the arm-swinging. It made me feel a little better.

"Also, during the other hours of the day when I felt angry at being a widow I promised myself to take it out against the world by doing the exercises tomorrow morning with fury. I promised myself that I would swing my arms with anger and with vigor and zest. This thought helped me get through the day."

"So, you found a way to shake your fist at the world!"

This clear labeling—and partial "working through" of Elizabeth's anger was the turning point in her therapy. We were able to terminate by the end of the seventh session.

The course of Elizabeth's therapy could be fairly summarized in brief fashion, as:

—mourner presents symptoms of repressed anger;

—counselor "reflects" and helps the mourner to identify and label her deep feeling;

—mourner is aided to recognize and express her deep anger;

—her fury erupts in words and behavior;

—her anger finds some release and her symptoms diminish.

How does *identifying and labeling* contribute to healing? In three dynamic ways:

—it clarifies;

—it provides a measure of meaning;

—it restores some of the mourner's self-esteem.

First, it guides the mourner in sorting out the jumble of his feelings. It teaches him to delineate, for his own clearer self-understanding, the separate threads in the mosaic of his emotional pain.

As we have described earlier, the mourner is beset with many fears and feelings. To be bereaved means to endure inner confusion, emotional vagueness, formless trauma. What he *clearly* feels is painful enough, what he *vaguely* feels can be even more distressing.

His emotional conflicts, ambivalences, and mood fluctuations trap him on a macabre merry-go-round of hopes, fears, yearnings, despair, dreams versus logic, and illusion versus reality. He'd love to jump off the whirling carousel, but can't see how to do it safely. He feels assaulted both by the intensity *and* the confusion of his emotions. He is enduring relentless pain that is ceaseless and unseizable, formless and mysterious.

When he is brought by the counseling transaction to an awareness that his fears *can* be named, he senses it as a partial relief, a slowing down of the whirling round and round. Identifying and labeling provides a handle-hold on an unreined runaway situation. At least now the mourner can take stronger bearings on the course of his emotional journey.

Secondly, it partially fills one of the mourner's principal needs, which is to discern some reason for his pain. As Victor Frankl has taught, the search for meaning is the core quest that lies at the center of man's struggle for spiritual wholeness and emotional peace of mind. The mourner feels more than pain and sadness—he feels *mocked by the senselessness and capriciousness* of this terrible event in his life.

He wishes he could find *some* purpose in his pain. Even a small meaning might give him a bit of comfort. It is the total mystery of death, the silence in the face of the riddle, that renders him helpless and rudderless, sinking without a compass in a stormy sea.

Identification and labeling of feeling is a step toward providing that compass. It is a move toward restoration of a sense of purpose and meaning. At least there is now a possibility that love is not a joke, that life is more than a cruel caprice.

Of course it is not the full answer that the mourner is searching for, but Band-Aids serve a purpose too. By cushioning the immediate pressure, a more comfortable situation is put together, from which the next step towards healing may be launched. It is an effective and useful deflector, albeit temporary, of sharp pain and puzzlement.

The *third* dynamic spurred by identification and labeling is the restoration of the mourner's pride in his own feelings and a deeper acceptance of his inner turmoil, despite its attendant pain. Labelling brings some semblance of order into a mourner's emotional chaos. It is a countermeasure to the negative distancing from painful emotions that mourners usually experience.

The bereaved person shuns his own pain and confusion. It is natural that he would wish to escape them. (His friends and family do so, why can't he?) He feels contaminated and diminished by his suffering. He hates his feelings and his entire being, his emotionally confining situation and his loneliness. He often slides into a general feeling of inferiority. He sees little positive about himself or his future.

The seemingly simple act of knowing what to call his pain, of being able to separate and identify its various components— fear of the future, anger, daydreaming, withdrawal, procrastination, guilt, imperfections of one degree or another—is a positive element in an otherwise negative situation. It is a recognizable feature and a touch of familiarity in an abnormal and strange environment.

It is a move away from the sense of inferiority that has been brought on by the necessity of enduring a distress that is vague and unnameable, toward a reality that is still cruel, but less mystifying. It is a small step, but a potentially significant one. It can be the opening of a door to a more endurable acceptance of reality.

In the counseling sessions, identification and labeling should not be presented as a simple exercise in language. It needs to be seen as much more than an unfeeling surgery of words or semantics. The counselor tries to lead the mourner, with empathy and urgency, on a journey of self-discovery of his own deeply imbedded emotions.

The counselor—who has by this time become a newly significant figure in the mourner's life—is in a better position to steer the mourner toward an honest identification of his deep feelings. It is an important step in the therapeutic process, and should be undertaken only by a trained bereavement counselor, and only in a structured setting.

The next two counseling techniques that we need to discuss—supporting, and assurance of normalcy—should not be conceived of as discrete or separate features of the counseling process. They are general approaches that the counselor recognizes as part of his fundamental perception of the process and that he can intertwine with all his other therapeutic interventions.

They are the skills that have been most directly drawn from the counselor's originally motivating empathy. They arise from genuine love and authentic empathy. Through training and practice a counselor can refine his general feeling of empathy into definable skills that are useful at almost every stage of the therapeutic process.

4. Assurance of Support

The central ingredient in the counselor's approach toward a troubled human being—a child of God—must be genuine empathy, unflagging support, evident concern. This is the sine qua non of bereavement counseling. Without it, success would be surprising; with it, failure should be rare and unexpected.

There are three ways through which a counselor can demonstrate personal support to the mourner: through attitude, through words, and through body language. Let us illustrate each area.

Attitude is the posture of the counselor's personality as he presents himself to the client. It is the unspoken framework of purpose, discipline, love, and experience within which the counselor sets up the therapeutic exchange. It presents, verbally and in other ways, the counselor's self-understanding of who he is and what he is about in attempting this enterprise with another human being.

It is projected through certain behavioral approaches, such as patience, tolerance, being nonjudgmental, establishing friendly rapport, assuring confidentiality. It expresses the counselor's open willingness to invest his time, intelligence, skill, and past life experience in the service of the mourner who is before him.

The counselor needs to demonstrate patience and tolerance. His purpose is not necessarily to direct the mourner to a new life. His purpose is to listen, to be with, to guide, to gently prod, to point suggestively to new insights. He needs to be patient with the mourner, to give him time for the struggle to find himself and to open up in expressing himself.

He needs to be patient with himself as he struggles to empathize. He needs to be patient as he debates within himself the best therapeutic course to follow, and goes about choosing the strategy and timing of his interventions.

Patience means pacing himself and the mourner to achieve the best possible results over a time period of eight counseling sessions, spanning 2 or 3 months. It means allowing for impreciseness on the part of the mourner and imperfections on the part of the counselor. Patience means not hurrying the journey, giving the process time to unfold, not expecting success on a strict schedule.

Tolerance means acceptance of whatever arises in the therapeutic transaction without anger, whether expected or unusual. Tolerance means allowing for trial and error and flexibility in the counseling strategy.

It signifies an ever-present readiness to accept, as worthy and significant, whatever the mourner expresses. Tolerance is what enables a counselor to practice his art with many mourners of different and diverse backgrounds.

A counselor needs to convey an implied assurance that he will not stand in judgment about any aspects of the mourner's life-style, sexual habits, prejudices, successes, or defeats. He is not there to condemn or impose any particular dogma, or to preach any article of faith, no matter how passionate his own conviction. He is not there primarily to "explain God."

His primary purpose, as we see it, is to support the mourner through a portion of his existential journey. He might be able to suggest some words of inspiration within the therapeutic parameters that we will discuss later; but that should never be his paramount aim.

The counselor's attitude of support can also be demonstrated by seeking to establish a friendly rapport. We recommend that bereavement counseling be done face-to-face—directly—with no desk intervening. All that is needed are two comfortable chairs and an empathic counselor who is able and willing to give his wholehearted attention to the mourner's needs while also being aware of his own. The usual politeness and courtesies are always in place, and a general spirit of pleasantness aids the therapeutic process.

Assurance of confidentiality should be assumed from the very beginning. If the mourner asks directly or if he appears hesitant to reveal private material, the counselor should unhesitatingly respond, "Yes, of course, these sessions are confidential, whatever you say to me will remain strictly between us." Therapy cannot proceed unless the client feels safe and absolutely secure that his privacy will be maintained.

This promise needs to be scrupulously carried out, even to the extent of avoiding casual mention of an appointment for counseling with an identifiable individual. Clergy especially should guard against seemingly inconsequential and untraceable remarks that they've been counseling individuals who may be identifiable in the local community.

The measure of support for the mourner is also connected to the extent of the counselor's willingness to invest his time and his intellectual and emotional energy. The counselor is offering significant skills and expending valuable know-how on behalf of another human being's welfare.

He should not make light of, even to himself, his contribution to a holy cause. He should be aware of, and take personal pride in, the "sacrifice" that he is offering. The more he accepts this notion, the greater the reservoir of competence he will be able to draw upon in marshalling and directing his empathic support for the bereaved person.

The counselor's decision and readiness to offer sustained support to the mourner derives from the clarity of his motive and the awareness of his purpose and goal. When the counselor in the process of preparing for his task is clear about his motives and connects them, through proper technique, to achieving a worthy and significant goal, one of the welcome by-products is a sustainable flow of support.

A genuine attitude of wanting to ease the mourner's pain, when it comes from the very fiber of the counselor's being, will penetrate to the core of the mourner's awareness. The mourner will experience it as an assurance of support that will greatly enhance the beneficial influence of the counseling.

Verbal support.   In the opening session, the counselor may have an opportunity to say, "We're going to try to help you. We have a program that has helped some people, and we hope it will help you too. Let's try, let's see. Tell me about your feelings, I will listen. I will try to understand what you are going through."

"Sometimes I feel so alone. Everyone says I'll get better, but they don't want to listen."

"That's one promise I can make, I'll listen and try to understand."

When the mourner is distressed and troubled by his feelings, the counselor may say, "It must be very painful, I can see that you're hurting. I'm very sorry that you're going through sadness (or loneliness—anger—being uninterested in life—feeling conflicts inside yourself—). I'm troubled for you, and I wish

I could take the pain away. It isn't easy for me but I'm trying to share the pain with you. I'll listen and I'll continue to listen during every session to anything that you want to express."

Verbal support is especially important when the mourner reaches the deeper level of "staying with" his painful emotions. The counselor may offer words in this vein: "It is important that you allow yourself to experience and "stay with" your feeling of anger (as an example). The best thing I can do for you is to encourage you to be aware of the feeling even if it hurts."

"Come, let's go through this together. Tell me about it—again and again, if you wish—you know I'll listen to you over and over if it's necessary. I'll read whatever you write down between sessions if you want me to. We'll go through sorrow together—as much as possible."

Nonverbal support. Empathy can be effectively demonstrated through nonverbal means as well as with words, and is aptly called body language. This can be very important in bereavement counseling, and is an additional benefit that can result from one-to-one counseling. It is less useful in group sessions.

The friendly atmosphere designed into Pastoral Bereavement Counseling, with direct opportunity for mutual emotional involvement and journeying, is a particularly appropriate setting for the effective use of body language.

We have found it very important to maintain steady and loving eye contact with the mourner. The eyes can become a channel for a two-way current of deep emotions. Steady and loving eye contact can express earnest involvement with the other, concern for the mourner's pain and interest in noting progress. An empathic gaze can be a declaration of caring friendship and unselfish love. Eye contact can be just as important as words.

Touch is a second nonverbal demonstration of support. To reach out and touch the other's hand, when it is done sincerely and openheartedly, can literally ease heartache. Often, while listening to a mourner, I have felt moved to lean forward to reach out and touch an arm or a hand.

Whenever I have done so as an expression of my heart, the

response clearly indicated that the sincerity was noticed and appreciated. The gesture of leaning forward, or of the touching of a hand, or both, is powerful and effective body language.

Equally powerful is for the counselor to permit himself to display his feelings when they have been stimulated by the release of the mourner's feelings. If you feel like crying *with* the mourner, our advice is not to hesitate, *provided your affect is real*.

The benefits of "crying with" arise from two factors. One, it is a powerful demonstration of your empathy and support. Two, it sends a message to the mourner, "It's okay to cry, it's okay to be aware of deep feeling, it's all right to release deep emotion." Both messages are central contributions to successful bereavement counseling.

5. Assurance of Normalcy

This is another general skill that is not used separately but together with the other techniques throughout the course of the counseling. It is conveyed by gentle suggestions that the normal bereavement process is usually a long journey, with many ups and downs and many to-be-expected twists and turns.

"I thought I was getting better, but the date of my husband's birthday brought back all of the painful memories. I can't stand all this rise of hope and then being dashed down to the pits again. I can't take too much more of this."

"Let's try to understand that this is not unusual—maybe it's part of the process. Things just don't happen on an even keel. From what you're telling me about your honest feelings, I wouldn't be too discouraged."

The counselor's readiness to transmit an assurance of essential normalcy should be based upon four clinical and structural factors:

1. a comprehensive *understanding of the dynamics* of the bereavement process and bereavement counseling, so that his perception of normalcy can be judged clinically valid;
2. unlimited and sustained *application of honest empathy*, so that the mourner will perceive the counselor's assurance as genuine;

3. having in place a functioning *system of clinical supervision* for the counselor-interns; and,
4. having in place a *network of mental health services* to which mourners who require further counseling may be reliably referred.

Assurance of normalcy should never be given lightly or perfunctorily, or as a device of "positive thinking." It should never be used as a cover-up for a counselor's ignorance or incompetence. If the counselor *isn't* convinced that the mourner is basically on a healthy track, he should not assure him, "This is normal."

How is a beginning counselor-intern to know if this particular client is basically normal? The answer is that no one can ever know for certain, even the most experienced counselor. However, our counselors will be meeting their responsibilities fully if they follow our design, use our recommended techniques, and stay within the therapeutic parameters we have outlined in this book.

This is also one of the issues that can be expected to be dealt with during the supervision process. One of the supervisors' tasks is to guide the counselor interns toward evaluating the rate of the mourner's progress (or lack of it) in relation to our model. Where too great a discrepancy becomes evident, the supervisors will not allow the counselor intern to assure normalcy.

This is why we do not recommend the establishment of a Pastoral Bereavement Counseling program unless arrangements are made to include responsible supervision. Wherever this component is an integral part of the program, even a beginning counselor will have a sufficient basis for a correct evaluation.

Our program's design includes a fail-safe mechanism which is an additional factor in enabling the counselor to assure a client's normalcy with confidence. This is the recommendation that communities arrange to make extended therapy available for those mourners who will need additional treatment beyond the eight sessions.

Fortified by ongoing clinical supervision, and with the knowledge that there is a backup, the counselor will have sufficient confidence in his estimate of the mourner's progress to give him a genuine assurance of normalcy.

For these reasons, the counselor will be able to offer an honest estimate of normalcy—always implicitly, always as a probability, never guaranteed—as part of his arsenal of techniques that are especially valid and useful in short-term therapy. He knows that if extended treatment becomes indicated as the process unfolds, he will be able to point the client toward further effective intervention. He will know that he has acted in good conscience not to harm his client.

Our experience indicates that assuring a mourner of his basic normalcy is of sufficient therapeutic value to have it reckoned as an important separate technique. As we see it, this assurance is more important to bereavement counseling than in general therapy, because mourners are often frightened by their unprecedented emotions—unprecedented in *their* lives. Their fears are aggravated because they have no prior experience in handling such feelings. Grief emotions are not only irrational, sometimes they take over the mourner's whole life —for days, for weeks, for months on end.

Mourners can become obsessed by their anger—withdrawal—guilt—to the extent that they fear for their sanity. The trauma is not only the actual pain, it is the irrational fear that the pains will never cease. They see no glimmer of light at the end of the darkness. They feel themselves sinking with no life preserver at hand.

In such a situation, being assured of basic normalcy can be a turning point. It can become an important part of the continuum of technique that forms the therapeutic response to these dark fears. It can give the troubled mourner a measure of hope—significant because it is given within a formal frame and structured setting—that in time they will probably move out of their rudderlessness and regain some measure of control.

To be effective, assurance of normalcy should be experienced only as part of an overall therapeutic process. It should be transmitted only in the manner we have suggested.

6. "Staying With"

"Staying with" is the counselor's therapeutic skill by which he guides the mourner's decision not to run away from the deep feelings that have begun to surface. It is the next step of the bereavement counseling experience, after the mourner has been brought to the imminent possibility that he will be able to recognize, confront, engage in, and wrestle with, his own deep feelings.

"Staying with" is the culmination of the continuum of therapeutic process that begins with dim stirrings of recognition of honest emotion (spurred by the counselor's use of reflection), continues with defining these emotions and bringing them into sharp focus (identification and labeling), and moves to the making of a conscious effort to turn one's full attention to these emotions ("staying with").

The next step, the one that will complete the therapy, will encourage the mourner to struggle to experience these emotions with all their nuances, ambivalences, and intensities, until their full disabling force will begin to dissipate ("working through").

The counselor's support and guidance in initiating the mourner into the experience of "staying with" is indispensable. No one is eager to enter into pain by themselves, let alone decide to confront and to endure it. Even the suggestion that it is healthy and potentially beneficial to "stay with" emotional discomfort doesn't make it easier.

It is only in a setting such as that provided by structured counseling, within an authentic relationship with a trusted figure who is seen as an appropriate confessor to whom may be revealed the sharpness of intimate pain, that the immersion into trauma can even be contemplated. "Staying with," for the counselor and mourner alike, requires courage and faith, and can be endured and "passed through" only within the context of a therapeutic relationship.

"What you're telling me is that you want me to be angry. But I don't *like* being angry, it disturbs me, it makes me mad. I'd rather feel something nice and pleasant. Why do I have to be angry?"

"No, you don't have to be angry. I'm not here to make you feel anything that isn't really in you. But if you *are* angry, if that's what you're *really* feeling, *I need you to know what you're feeling*. If you feel cheated because Henry died, I think you should express it—right now—if that's what you're feeling—say it—I'm angry, I feel cheated."

"What good will it do?"

"That's not the point. I want to you to express whatever you're feeling because I know it will be good for you. Listen to me, do you think I'm trying to help you?"

"Yes."

"Well, then try to do what I'm asking. If you're feeling anger, or want to strike out, or hate God or someone, or feel like cursing—recognize that you're angry—say it out loud—or at least, whisper it to yourself—say it, I'm angry!"

"What good will it do?"

"It's a step in the process. It's one of the steps I think you'll have to travel through—sooner or later. I think it'll be easier if you can travel through while you have me to listen to you."

"Yes, I suppose it would be easier that way—but I don't want to—it's very difficult—I'd rather not—it's not right to be angry."

"It's not right to be angry all the time, but it's okay if you're angry some of the time—if you're feeling that way now, or if you'll be angry during the coming week. And especially if you'll tell me about it. I'm going to ask you about what you've been feeling during our next session."

"Staying with" also means that the counselor seeks to design strategies to evoke in the mourner the reexperiencing of his deep emotions, whether painful or not. He makes plans to try to lead the mourner to reiterate the expressions and descriptions of his feelings again and again, as long as therapeutically necessary.

The counselor stays on the alert to use every opportunity that presents itself during subsequent counseling session to prod the mourner to reexpress his feelings, even if similar sentiments were already touched. This leads directly into the next stage of the mourner's journey.

7. "Working Through"

"Working through" is the sequel to "staying with." It is the continued and sustained engagement with the primal emotions of grief. In "staying with," the mourner has focused on his deep emotions and has begun to pay attention to them with intensity and as undeviatingly as possible. As the process continues, this earnest contemplation of primal emotion—"working through"—triggers certain mechanisms, both conscious and unconscious, that break down and digest these emotions and separate them into subcomponents.

As the "working through" continues, these subcomponents are integrated into new combinations, so that the emotional configuration is modified, and the mourner begins to live in a changed psychological context. In time, this sustained wrestling produces a different psychological orientation, an old-new emotional ambience which permits the mourner to be less obsessed with his past loss. This changed pattern of feeling and perception allows him to be more comfortable with his present challenges and his hopes for the future. This is the "turning of the corner" in his journey through grief.

This has been the natural process of adjustment to grief from time immemorial. * The Pastoral Bereavement Counselor aims to facilitate this natural process, to keep it in motion, on course, to remove any obstacles or fixations that may arise, to guide and support the mourner through the difficulties of experiencing pain, and to monitor his progress through a portion of his overall journey.

---

*It may be that the ceremonies, rites, and customs, both religious and cultural, that developed around burial and postburial practices in past human societies, were rooted in these natural mechanisms. This is a subject worthy of extensive investigation, but would take us too far afield from this book's area of concern.

While our present purpose is primarily practical and pragmatic—how to set up a service in each community to heal a mourner's wounds—it is possible that a by-product of our movement might be a heightened sensitivity among the general public to the natural processes of mourning. This could ultimately modify some of our contemporary funeral and postfuneral practices.

"Working through" is, in a sense, the summation of the mourner's task, towards which all the prior techniques and sub-processes have been preparing, and from which it is hoped that a modified way of perceiving and facing the future will evolve. It can lead to "turning the corner" from incapacitating sorrow to a reality-facing way of life. It is the operative detail of the natural miracle of adjustment that our counselors can contribute to and witness close-up.

During the counseling sessions the Pastoral Bereavement Counselor facilitates the "working through" process in three ways: by his evident personal faith in and professional acceptance of the validity of the process; by his application of counseling technique to encourage the mourner to enter the process; and by planning strategy to give the "working through" process time to take hold.

First, the counselor must be personally convinced of the importance and validity of "working through," and must appreciate its central and helpful role. Only then will he be able to utilize his basic empathy to firmly lead the mourner into a valley of pain.

"I'm surprised that you're asking me to endure pain. I thought your counseling would take the pain away."

"We hope that our program will be able to help you,* but we're taking an indirect route. We believe that in the long run it's the healthier and better way. It's part of the journey you have to travel, to go through certain emotions that you will recognize within yourself. We've spoken earlier in these sessions of the journey that many mourners go through, and this is part of that journey."

"I think you're trying to help me, otherwise I wouldn't be

---

*In this instance, the counselor chose a positive directive response, because his immediate purpose at this point in the counseling process was to move the mourner into "working through." If he had felt that the mourner's remark denoted some growing resistance and wanted to probe that possibility, he would have chosen a reflective response, such as, "Are you disappointed in our program? Were you expecting something else?" The counselor tries to be open to the different interventions possible at any stage, and chooses one of several possible alternatives.

here. But it's very painful, I don't understand how this is going to help."

"Well, it has helped others, we're trying to do the same for you. It really does make sense to take it step by step. And remember, it's not pain in general that we're asking you to feel, it's something specific that I'm asking you to tell me—what's going on inside of you. When you recognize some feeling, whatever it is—you remember?—you mentioned something about being angry—when you feel it, tell me about it—stay with that feeling, talk to me about it—or write it down. We think it's a healthy thing to do."

Second, certain counseling techniques are very useful in introducing the mourner to the process of "working through." They can help him to sustain a focus on his difficult emotions. We have already described the counseling skills most useful for the opening sessions—listening, reflecting, clarifying, and identifying and labeling. Two additional techniques will take the counselor into the process of "working through" with the mourner:

1. alertness to cues to the mourner's emotional depths; and
2. asking for details of the mourner's daily living patterns.

The first suggests that the counselor watch for references or allusions to an emotion that had been previously broached, seemingly forgotten for one or two sessions, and then casually surfaces again. The counselor should pick up on these cues. He should try to use them as springboards to return the mourner's attention to a primal emotion and to intensify that attention into a "working through."

Another counseling technique that draws the mourner's focus to his deep emotions and that can serve as an opening to a process of "working through" is to inquire about how he spends his time. What are his usual activities? How does she spend her day?"

The counselor asks for details and, in listening carefully to the responses, can usually discern the dominant emotions that are filling the mourner's days and nights. When these feelings are pointed out, a vantage point is opened for the mourner to increase his self-awareness and self-understanding.

This technique is very useful, and with some mourners can be effectively utilized for "working through." Indeed, one of the signals that this phase is concluding is when the mourner speaks along these lines: "I see that you're asking me again for details about what I did yesterday. I know what you want me to do, you want me to go through my guilt feelings again. I'm not sure it's necessary, I know what I'm feeling."

The counselor will also be able to recognize the other sign of a movement towards the conclusion of the therapy: a diminution of the urgency the mourner displays in expressing his feelings. In some instances, the mourner will recognize it himself and say so directly. "You know, I don't need to talk about my anger so much anymore." In other instances, the counselor will notice that the mourner is simply omitting mention of the troubling subjects that he felt compelled to bring up in earlier sessions. The counselor silently notes that the mourner has moved on to other material.

In such cases, if the mourner also reports fewer functional problems and seems to be returning to normal pre-loss behavior, the counselor might suggest that it is time to think about concluding the therapy.

Changes in the emotional content of the mourner's life, *and* normal functional behavior (eating, sleeping, work habits, etc.), *and* no new somatic disturbances are the best sign that our program's goal has been reached. The sessions should then be terminated even prior to the eight-week maximum.

8. Noting and Commending Every Sign of Progress

The counselor should not wait for complete healing before pointing out partial progress to the mourner. His notice and commendation of *any* advance in the mourner's journey, no matter how small, is important enough to be categorized as a significant counseling technique.

This is because, as we have described earlier, the mourner's problem is not only a specific ailment, but fear in general. Bereaved people are at the mercy of a vague terror, an unnamable distress that is, for most grievers, unprecedented in their lives.

They feel themselves standing on such a weak emotional

and psychological footing that they've lost confidence in their ability to cope. Even a slight improvement in accomplishing their normal tasks, when noted and commented upon by the new significant figure in their life—their bereavement counselor—can be a powerful and energizing psychological vitamin.

This eighth listing in our recommended counseling techniques can be seen as an extension into the middle and later sessions of the fourth and fifth, assurance of support, assurance of normalcy, that we viewed as so important for the opening sessions.

As the counseling proceeds, as the counselor and mourner together "stay with" and continue to "work through," *some* progress will take place. (If there is *no* visible change, the full situation should be brought to the supervisor's attention without delay. It may be an indication that immediate referral to more intensive treatment is advisable.) But it is essential that that measure of progress be noted by the counselor and that the mourner be commended. This intervention acts as a powerful restorer of the mourner's self-confidence. When *every* opportunity for applauding the mourner's progress is taken, the griever's coping powers can be exponentially strengthened and more quickly restored.

In the early sessions, the widow, Wilma, spoke of her fears of losing her sanity.

"What's the matter with me, I can't concentrate, my only thoughts are on how much I miss John. Yesterday it took me six hours to clean my apartment. In every room I just sat in the chair, with dustcloth in hand, and cried and remembered. I just don't know where the day went."

"You were remembering and crying . . . "

"I couldn't keep my mind on anything else—six hours of dusting furniture! What's going to become of me!"

Three sessions later, Wilma seemed to be a little better, but her emerging guilt feelings were preventing her from acknowledging the progress directly.

"I'd be interested to hear. What are some of the things you've been doing in the last few days?"

"Well, Monday is cleaning day. It's still taking me too long. I spent the whole morning dusting my apartment and watering the plants."

"The whole morning? About how many hours?"

"Right after breakfast and after a few phone calls . . . I suppose it took about two-and-a-half hours . . . When am I going to get back to normal?"

"Wilma, that's terrific! two-and-a-half hours, that's progress! . . . seems to me you're doing better."

"That's not better, it should take a half hour at most."

"But it's better than you were doing three weeks ago. Do you remember, you told me it took some six hours."

Wilma paused, struggling with whether to accept the commendation or argue.

The counselor hurried to take the opportunity to follow up: "But it's clearly better—you're making good progress. You're crying less, and daydreaming less. I think it's much better. You haven't yet gone all the way, but you've moved a good distance. I'm proud of you!"

The counselor should not hesitate to make a fuss about even slight progress. When we witness a person beginning to climb up out of the valley of sadness, we should show our gratification for them. We believe it is legitimate for us to want to transmit that uplift of spirit to the mourner, especially when they are in the midst of the "working through" process.

Our experience indicates that noting and commending, when applied in a timely fashion, is highly effective.

9. Words of Faith, Poetry, Philosophy

The counselor may, after the process of "working through" has taken hold, offer inspirational words or spiritual concepts, *when* and *if* the mourner invites them or otherwise indicates his readiness for them.

The words or ideas should be offered gently and sincerely, as a demonstration of friendship and an implementation of the counselor's empathy.

The ideas should be put forward as suggestions, as a thought to explore, never as an imposition of doctrine or with an air of insistence.

The counselor's unspoken attitude should be: "My dear friend, at this point in our mutual efforts to deal with your sorrow and mankind's sadness, I'd like to share some ideas, some faith or philosophy that I'm comfortable with and that has helped me. I believe that this has helped others in past generations too, and represents the accumulated wisdom of generations on this difficult subject."

"I offer these thoughts freely to you, perhaps they can help you too. But if they can't, you're under no obligation to accept them to please me. Perhaps knowing about them will plant a seed of something worthwhile in your life. Perhaps you will nurture and develop them in your own fashion. Perhaps they will become meaningful to you, too."

The counselor should choose only that philosophy or poem or word of comfort that he believes in personally. The counseling site is not a pulpit. It is appropriate to discuss ritual only insofar as it reflects or bears upon the mourner's feelings. The counselor may offer words of faith, but should not set up a contest of creeds.

The mourner should feel no pressure to be convinced, and must be allowed to explore his own thoughts and feelings. He is to be permitted to question and to disagree, even as the counselor permits himself that freedom.

In a counseling situation, where honest feeling commingles with logical thought, the only healthy certainties are those that are freely accepted and have been freely worked through. Within these parameters, faith, philosophy, and poetry may be useful tools for our program.

It is important for our counselors to appreciate why philosophy and words of inspiration can be helpful only if introduced after the "working through" process has commenced. To begin earlier would be counterproductive at best and dangerous at worst. The first need for mourners is for someone to validate and legitimize their feelings. Above all, they need to feel instinctively sure that someone is genuinely interested in listening to and sharing some of their pain.

The last thing they need is for someone to put up a wall and to say, in effect, "Your feelings are not my concern. I'm going to protect myself from your pain by giving you high-sounding advice. (It's rather easy for me to do this, because it's only surface advice, I haven't really struggled through to it through my own experiences, and I don't want to struggle through to it.)

That will make me feel wise and important, and will get me off the hook as far as helping you is concerned."

Without the counselor being intentionally heartless, this is what advice-giving and inspirational platitudes can sound like to the mourner's inner ear. This can turn off any possibility of developing the kind of helpful relationship that the mourner desperately needs. If a griever has a succession of such encounters, it can only intensify his sense of aloneness and increase his despair.

Inspiration and philosophy for mourners are potentially harmful when mistakenly used as first-aid measures. They can only be helpful when used as support during the convalescing phase. It is only *after* the deep feelings—at least some of them—have been honestly engaged and unflinchingly confronted that the time may be propitious for words of comfort.

At that time the counselor is in a position to reinforce the process of emotional "working through" by words of faith, philosophy, or poetry. This technique, at the appropriate time, can propel the griever further along his journey, and increase his speed on the road to healing.

As to the choice of texts, each counselor may choose, from his own religious sources or cultural background, those phrases or concepts that have *appealed to him in his own wrestling* with personal bereavement or fears of mortality. They are offered in a spirit of intimate empathy.

"These ideas have helped me in my wrestling with my dark fears, perhaps they may be useful to you. Perhaps you'll allow them to affect you, remembering all the deep feelings we have shared in the counseling sessions up till now. Knowing you as I do, I think they might fit your needs. I offer them to you as another seal on the bond of our friendship."

10. Therapeutic Termination

How do we know when to conclude the sessions? What are the therapeutic factors to consider in seeking to effect a healthy termination of bereavement counseling? How do we refer for further treatment when necessary?

From the very start, the counselor should keep firmly in

mind the basic design of the limitation of "up to eight sessions." As we have previously discussed, the built-in short-term aspect achieves two purposes: it concentrates the intellectual and emotional energies of all concerned towards a central focus; and it reduces the potential for dependence and countertransference. These two factors, although largely in the background of the counselor's attention during most of the sessions, become more important in planning the last phase.

About 70 percent of the mourners who have been serviced by our New York program have gone through the full eight sessions. The remaining number terminated after four to seven sessions; one moved to a therapeutically justifiable termination during the first and only interview.

In all of these situations, three issues emerged around the process of termination:

1. dealing with the measure and the quality of the mourner's dependence on the counselor that was aroused during the course of therapy;
2. the extent to which either the griever or counselor reacts to the scheduled termination as a partial bereavement; and
3. reviewing and evaluating the course of the counseling.

As previously discussed, the program of Pastoral Bereavement Counseling should be described as a "maximum of eight sessions" in all the announcements of the service to the community.* In addition, the short-term aspect of the program is further clarified in the intake procedures and in the initial counseling session. It is also generally useful to refer matter-of-factly to the *number* of each upcoming session when scheduling or confirming it.

Nevertheless, it is not uncommon, as the eighth session approaches, for the mourner to express some feelings about the upcoming separation, and it is best to give the griever an opportunity to describe his anxiety. The counselor should state clearly that the Pastoral Bereavement Counseling Program in

---

*Samples of suggested copy are available at the New York office of the Commission on Pastoral Bereavement Counseling.

their community adheres strictly to the maximum eight-session agreement. If the mourner in the future should come to feel a strong need to resume sessions, he should once again contact the local coordinator, not the counselor who has conducted the original sessions. In each community, the clinical Director, after consultation with the Counselor or Supervisor, will be in a position to decide whether and how to refer the mourner for further counseling.

Secondly, we should recognize that it is natural, for both mourner and counselor, to experience a certain sadness at the prospect of no longer meeting and sharing together. After all, a genuine friendship has been forged, emotional intimacies have been shared, fears and hopes have been acknowledged, significant insights have been exchanged. After 8 hours of soul-searching conversation it would be a sign of emptiness and sterility if the end brought no regrets.

The counselor allows the mourner to express such sentiments. He may acknowledge that he harbors similar feelings, and that they are to be expected. He should however be alert to the possibility that *some* mourners may be feeling a greater dependency.

They may express lingering difficulty in contemplating the end of the counseling relationship. "I still feel sad, I still cry at night, and I can't seem to get a hold of myself. Can't you make an exception and see me a few more times?"

Or, "I feel so much better when I can look forward to our weekly meetings. I'd like very much to see you one more time. You're helping me a great deal."

The basic counselor response to such a statement would be along these lines: "Progress in adjusting to bereavement is not in a straight line, usually it goes through many ups and downs. We've seen examples of that during these weeks.

"But you have improved, haven't you? Overall, you're better than you were a few weeks ago. [Cite specific illustrations.] So you know now that it is possible to improve. I think it's probable that you'll continue to improve. As for my seeing you, our program is designed in a certain way to achieve a certain limited goal, and I think we've pretty much reached that goal.

"If you think you need more counseling I'd like to explore

that feeling with you a little deeper—I'd like us both to understand why you're feeling that way. After we talk about it, and if you'll still feel that you want to arrange for more sessions, I'll refer you for additional treatment.

"I appreciate that you think well of me, but actually *you've* done the hard work, *you* have faced your honest feelings, and *that's* what has really helped you. So I think you deserve more credit than anyone else, and you should be confident that you'll continue your progress."

This is another opportunity for the counselor to bring his natural empathy into play. He is in the best position to understand and sympathize with the mourner's reluctance to let go. He also understands how necessary it is, and he can use both his heart and mind, he can blend his professional firmness and empathic sensitivity, in implementing the termination phase.

Part of the reason the griever shows reluctance to end the counseling is due to the phenomenon of transference (a logically unexplainable nexus of feelings towards a person or situation that is inappropriate to the reality of the relationship or the objective circumstances of the situation, and that is derived from deeply imbedded and highly influential past experiences.) The mourner, having recently endured the loss of a loved one may—illogically but overridingly—perceive the end of counseling as another severe blow to his emotional equilibrium. The counselor has, over the past few weeks, become a new significant figure in his sorry life—perhaps the griever's main crutch.

Under the circumstances, no matter what the original "contract" with the counselor was, the end of counseling means yet another grievous loss, another door of hope slammed shut in his face. He may be beset with feelings that characterize a loss due to death, similar to the illogical anger, guilt, and fantasizing that he felt in the aftermath of the first loss.

The counselor may have become a substitute beloved figure for the actual beloved who died a few months ago. The end of the counseling sessions might trigger another full-blown bereavement reaction. The counselor may find it necessary to attempt to work through this feeling in one or two of the last sessions.

If the mourner continues to express excessive dependency,

it should be discussed with the supervisor with an eye to considering recommendation for further therapy. But the rule that is structured into the design of Pastoral Bereavement Counseling should be strictly followed—the original counselor does not go further than eight sessions with the mourner.

What has been our experience with the mourners who terminated at less than eight? What are the signs that make earlier termination possible and justifiable? We suggest that the counselor look for one of two criteria that can manifest themselves during short-term therapy.

The first is to recognize movement or change in the emotional content of the mourner's words and behavior. The second is when the counselor discerns in the mourner an improved self-acceptance of his emotions and a lessening of the urgency to unburden himself. When the mourner reports different emotions in the later sessions than those he had been obsessed with earlier, if he ventilates with less urgency, and if at least one of the primal emotions has been "worked through," it should be perceived as significant movement and genuine progress.

The counselor then has fulfilled his goal of helping the mourner take his first step(s) in his journey through bereavement. When the griever-client realizes that he has turned a corner, and the counselor concurs, it becomes therapeutically justifiable to conclude the program prior to the eighth session.

The counseling techniques for a therapeutic termination include a review and evaluation of the emotional movement that has taken place, a labeling of the emotions that were uncovered and explored, and a summation of the results achieved.

The counselor can ask such questions as: "Well, what has happened during these weeks? Do you remember what you were thinking and talking about when you first came? What feelings have you gone through during these weeks? Do you remember any turning points? Are you now on an even keel, or are you having ups and downs? What about the future? What would you guess about your future feelings?"

In the terminating phase, the counselor should not do much talking. He should listen to the mourner's replies to these questions and similar proddings. He can learn from this material and gain experience to use in counseling his next mourner.

Termination procedures usually take less than a session, sometimes as little as 10 minutes. But they are important to implement; they should not be overlooked. They constitute the summation of the therapeutic encounter.

They can function as the "period, paragraph," as a link between the past and the future, or even as the newest chapter heading in the mourner's life odyssey. They can become an important learning experience for the counselor as well.

For both mourner and counselor, a proper therapeutic termination is the signature, the "Sincerely and affectionately yours," of a significant document in both their lives.

SUMMATION: THESE TEN AND THESE TEN ONLY

Having completed this discussion of the counseling techniques we recommend for Pastoral Bereavement Counseling, 10 in all, we should mention a number of caveats. First, our purpose here was not to provide a training manual, nor to recommend specific instructions for every particular situation.

Our purpose was to present a model of the theory and practice of Pastoral Bereavement Counseling, derived from the clinical observations we have compiled during our 12 years of working with mourners. We believe that this model represents an effective and therapeutically valid design for providing a new community service for mourners. We have packaged it and introduced it in New York, and we would welcome invitations to establish it in other communities.

The Training Course involves a minimum of 12 hours of instruction, the supervisors should be given a few hours of orientation, and the internship program needs to be conducted for a period of 1 to 2 years before Pastoral Bereavement Counselors can become fully certified.

We recognize that, even then, the art of structured bereavement counseling will never be able to be completely standardized. There will be as many different variations, emphases and nuances, in how this activity will ultimately be practiced, as there are many different clergy, social workers, nurses, and supervisors in each community. No two counselors will practice Pastoral Bereavement Counseling in exactly the same manner.

The model that has been presented in this book is not hewn from stone, and is of course open to amendment and further clinical refinement. It is meant to be seen as a presentation of a pioneer concept, combining well-known techniques in an innovative package, cognizant of all the relevant dynamic factors, and seeking to anticipate some of the legitimate questions that might be raised. It is our hope that clergy and others who hear about our movement will become interested in undertaking the necessary training and clinical supervision that would qualify them for service in this field.

We believe that Pastoral Bereavement Counseling is uniquely useful because of a second aspect of our set of techniques. This uniqueness does not derive from the methods themselves, which are well-known to counselors, especially of the Rogerian school. But it is the exclusive combination of these techniques—these 10 and no others—that produces effective healing for mourners in a relatively short period of time.

At different stages of the therapeutic process the counselor will use his judgment in selecting one or the other of these techniques as most appropriate for that stage; but at no point is there need or justification for using any other technique. The optimum results are obtainable by using these 10 exclusively—in this case, adding is subtracting. Our counselors will need to be trained not only to employ these 10 skills, but to deny themselves the option of using any other. They are asked to unlearn the traditional approaches that will serve them adequately in their other roles and relationships, but to adopt "our 10" when they serve as bereavement counselors.

Pastoral Bereavement Counselors should always be checking on themselves during and after each session, (or, the supervisors may inquire), "Which of the 10 techniques were being employed?" This is an effective way, especially for clergy in the counseling situation, to wean themselves from preachment and exhortation. These approaches stand them in good stead in their functioning in other professional situations, but they have no place in bereavement counseling.

The 10 techniques we recommend for Pastoral Bereavement Counselors form a discrete and self-contained package. For healing mourners, they are the counseling methods that are necessary and sufficient. For the Pastoral Bereavement Counselor, they are the sole means he may use for reaching his goal.

The Pastoral Bereavement Counselor expects that by establishing a goal-directed relationship with the grief-stricken mourner, by helping him confront and identify his pain, by empathically enduring his anguish with him, by encouraging his every sign of normal functioning, and by being alert to any sign of abnormal reactions, he will succeed in moving the mourner through the valley towards restored health.

These 10 techniques, when put into operation within the framework of our structured design, have the potential of shortening the duration of the mourner's experience of deep trauma. They can increase the velocity of the bereaved's passage through those episodes of deep distress that mourning necessarily entails. They can function as the mechanisms that enable an empathic counselor to accompany a suffering mourner through the valley of the shadow. They enable the counselor to stay with the mourner till he moves to the beginning of the return ascent.

Chapter 8

CAN THIS CLAIM BE TRUE?

I must confess that I found it difficult to put on paper the words of the previous chapter. It sounds preposterous to claim that the 10 counseling techniques, used within the structured design, constitute a formula that produces healing for a mourner's wounds. I am painfully aware that my claims can be dismissed as the product of hysterical delusion or ego-driven arrogance.

"Can it actually be," I hear some readers asking, "that this author really believes he has discovered a new and effective remedy for the pains of grief that have burdened mankind from time immemorial? Isn't this what all religious leaders and all the wise men of the ages have sought for millennia—and whose efforts have met with only partial success? Isn't it preposterous for him to believe that he has succeeded where everyone before him has failed?"

To a reader with such a thought I would try to respond, yes, it sounds arrogant and unbelievable, quite preposterous and overreaching. Yet, I cannot deny my life's experience, nor find any glaring faults in the system we've named Pastoral Bereavement Counseling. During the 12 years since its inception, throughout all the counseling, training, and supervision, there has not been a single week in which I haven't witnessed direct evidence of its benefits.

As unbelievable as the claim sounds when placed in cold type, I am forced to the conclusion that the method is effective and helpful in the overwhelming majority of cases. In this book I have attempted to describe the theoretical underpinnings of the skills and techniques I recommend, and the dynamic rationale that justifies their selection and explains their success. I eagerly look forward to other practitioners adopting these methods and, working within the safeguards I have suggested, coming forward to report their results.

Let us temper the boldness of our assertion—but with no softening of our claim for effectiveness—by addressing two clarifications to the skeptical reader.

Not a Cure, but a Healing

The first is to disabuse ourselves of the notion that we are effecting a *cure* for grief. Indeed, a claim of that nature *would* be preposterous. It would be naive, unrealistic and false. To hope in such terms might become a danger and an entrapment for the mourner. Clearly, we make no such claim.

We do not claim to *cure*, in the sense of eliminating pain. Pastoral Bereavement Counselors hope to *heal*, to leave less of a scar, to shorten the experience of pain. Absolute cure from grief would be palpably unnatural. Would it have been right for God to so constitute human nature as to make it easy for us to shrug off the loss of a true love?

It would be a mockery of the intensity and cosmic significance of human affection to expect its termination to leave no mark. To expect such a cure would transform our life's love into a cruel illusion. Such a "cure" would ultimately be worse than the "disease."

We see a more reasonable purpose to our efforts—and more clearly attainable. Our aim is not to *eliminate* pain, but to *smooth the passage* through pain.

Our methods make the pain more comfortable to deal with,

the distress less stressful. Our counseling techniques serve their purpose maximally when they chart a passage through the mourner's feelings that will lead him to a safe harbor. We do not try to skirt the storm, we install emotional stabilizers so that the griever will be less seasick.

We provide a healing, not a cure. Our aim may be bold, but it is reachable. It may sound arrogant, but it should not be judged preposterous. We ask the skeptical reader to give our program a fair chance. Let's ask ourselves, which is really more preposterous and presumptuous—the old informal way, or our pioneering structured system? I'm beginning to think that the traditional posture of clergy towards mourners is the more preposterous one.

Sometimes I wonder how intelligent and sincere clergy have for so long deluded themselves into thinking that informal ministrations—or even words of preachment—are appropriate to or commensurate with the mourner's trauma.

How could we have expected it to be such an easy process? Isn't it highly unreasonable to imply, as our miniscule efforts do, that a few hours or a few days after the funeral is sufficient time to say good-bye to a marriage of 35 or 40 years? Or to a parental, or sibling, or any other loving relationship?

Should we really expect the surviving husband or wife to quickly erase the memory of a lifetime of spousal companionship and conjugal relationship? So many shared struggles and dreams, so many discrete and myriad instances of emotional bonding—is it healthy to sweep all this under the rug of forgetfulness or escape?

Isn't it preposterous for us to so relate to grievers that we stifle their legitimate rebellion against God's justice—with platitudes and preachment and philosophy—with anything *but* empathy? Especially for clergy, whose choice of vocation was presumably connected to a felt need within us to grapple all our lives with seeking to understand God's ways?

Wouldn't it be right for us to be involved with our flock's wrestling with God during a supreme grief in their lives? And not just for a moment, or for an hour, or just during the funeral?

And, if we grudgingly grant that mourning is a lengthy and arduous travail, why have we not given it some semblance of sustained attention? Why have we not, until now, developed a serious and consistent approach to dealing with this problem? This is what Pastoral Bereavement Counselors set out to do, this is why we claim to be pioneers.

THE TRUE ARROGANCE

Maybe *we* are not the arrogant ones. Perhaps those who make it sound so simple and easy are the ones who are arrogant and unfeeling. If we appear to be somewhat arrogant, at least we seek to deal with the problem with some sensitivity and some responsibility. We'd rather be bold and accountable than insensitive and irresponsible.

Are we serving God if we hide from the mourner's panic and pain that we should know *necessarily* follows a funeral? Are we serving God when we flee from being ourselves emotionally touched? Can we be responsible shepherds without looking for ways to share the pain?

Why should we expect the event that for many in our flock is life's most serious and enduring problem, to be ameliorated by words that are eminently logical but thunderingly irrelevant to the sufferer?

I turn to my "skeptical" colleagues who may be asking, "Can this claim be true?" with a straightforward appeal. "Try it. Undertake to do it. Learn the method. Offer your life's experience and professional skill and personal empathy to those who most need it. Undertake to actually counsel a mourner, and open yourself to being supervised."

If your experience will be anything like mine and those of other counselors, a whole new world of altruistic service will open up to you. Just possibly, there might arise in your religious consciousness a clearer affirmation of what your career may mean in God's eyes.

Consider, before you judge our claim, whether or not an improvement is called for in the way clergy—and most of our society—responds to the mourner's wounds. The methods that have been utilized until now have been nothing more than a postponement of pain. At best, they are nothing more than a delay or a dilution of the necessary natural process.

This is the unavoidable, if unintended result of such advice as, "Why don't you take a vacation!" "Try to keep busy," "Go out and meet new people," or "Pick up the threads of your life."

Other advice in the commonly used approach is even more damaging. "Keep it out of your mind—Be brave—Smile and the world smiles with you—He'd want you to carry on—Life is too short to waste time grieving—Time will heal—" is a sweeping under the rug and a thwarting of the natural process. It is a denial of the pain that sooner or later must be faced. It can hurt the mourner by delaying the healthy wrestling that is needed.

What it comes down to, if you wish to judge our claim, is whether or not you are satisfied with the present state of affairs. Those who are, will judge our movement to be arrogant and superfluous. Those who seek improvement may welcome our approach and judge it worthy of serious consideration. To them, we offer our experience and our suggestions, our structured design, and our ten counseling techniques.

The second clarification is to suggest to all would-be Pastoral Bereavement Counselors to apply only the ten recommended techniques—those and no other. The efficacy of our method is best demonstrated when other techniques are not allowed to interfere.

But, of course, applying these techniques and eschewing all others is easier planned than performed. It entails not only learning the new methods, but also *un*learning the usual approaches that have become so ingrained as to have become our unconscious modus operandi.

Our Commission has established minimum standards for certification as Pastoral Bereavement Counselors. Among these are successful completion of a 12-hour Training Course, and the carrying through of 10 counseling situations under clinical supervision. We do not recommend clergy or other mental health practitioners to undertake Pastoral Bereavement Counseling sessions without following that path.

It takes long practice, under competent supervision, to refrain from giving easy advice, to be consistently empathic, to feel internal resonance to another's pain, to "stay with" sorrow, and to trust one's instincts in a counseling situation. The claim we make may sound arrogant on paper, but it is a very humbling experience in the flesh.

We believe that our methods will be proven effective and reliable when they are correctly and consistently applied. We look forward to the time when our movement will have expanded to the point where it can be scientifically tested and evaluated.

Another reason that we make the claim that Pastoral Bereavement Counseling is superior to previous methods of helping mourners is to draw attention to its radical difference. It is not an alteration of, or interference with, the natural process of mourning, as the usual methods turn out to be. Just the opposite, it is an intensification of and a riveting of the mourner's attention to the natural process of mourning. This is the core of its dynamic effectiveness.

PARTNERS WITH GOD

Pastoral Bereavement Counseling lubricates the engine that God has set up to move the mourner to health and healing, by adding a blend of a counselor's empathy and technical skills. It is not a diversion from the mourner's task. It is an empathic prodding to the mourner to get on with his or her task.

It is neither avoidance nor sugarcoating of the pain of grief. It is a counselor's participation with and accompaniment of the mourner through a significant portion of the grief journey. Pastoral Bereavement Counseling is different and effective because it directs the mourner to deal intensely with his deep feelings in a radical yet empathic manner.

Our bereavement counseling system puts the counselor in the position of suggesting to the mourner, gently, but with a sense of earnestness, "You probably recognize, deep down, that you cannot escape the pain. You can only hope to pass through it without permanent damage. If you're willing to try, I'd like to try with you. Will you accept my offer to be your harbor pilot, as together we search for the best channel to safety?"

Can our claim be true? We believe it is!

Precisely because of its radical difference, precisely because Pastoral Bereavement Counseling takes the long view of the bereavement process, precisely because it does not pander to the short-term desires of the griever to find easy surcease from emotional pain, precisely because it allows neither mourner nor counselor to succumb to the facile attraction of surface philosophy—just because it is contrary to the accepted notions—we have seen that our claim is true and that our system produces beneficial results.

Our own encouragement and conviction arises from the evidence of progress we have seen in the hundreds of cases that our Commission has processed. We have seen the preponderant majority clearly helped. We have not therapeutically injured any of the bereaved persons who have come to our program. Even in those instances where progress was limited, or where the prior history of the mourner complicated his recovery, follow-up reports months later bore testimony to the value and benefits of our intervention.

We are proud to cite a brief statement by one of our clients, which summarizes his perception of how he was helped. Although in this instance we treated the mourner at a later stage than most of our cases, we selected this report because of its brevity and clarity.

Timothy, a young man in his late twenties, felt distressed about his mother's death twenty-six months earlier. He had sought help with three other therapists but still felt troubled. He had been recommended to our program by one of our former clients. At the opening of the fifth session he surprised the counselor with a very positive statement which indicated such great progress that the counselor suggested this might be the last session.

"Let's explore how your feelings have changed in the last few weeks. If we both agree that you don't need any more sessions, let's make this the last one."

Twenty minutes later, it became evident that Timothy had navigated a successful passage through the normal bereavement emotions, that there seemed to be no unfinished grieving business that he wouldn't be able to handle on his own, and that no further counseling sessions were needed.

The counselor expressed gratification at this happy turn of events, and asked Timothy if he could summarize the course of the therapy. This is what Timothy sent in a few days later.

1-29-87

> After my fourth session I felt as if I had been reborn. Everything seemed to make sense and I felt that there was a future for me. I understood my feelings and could express my anger without feeling guilty. I also had no guilt feelings about wanting to enjoy myself. The counselor helped me realize that I am allowed to enjoy and begin a new chapter in my life. I can turn the corner and keep on walking. I still go back into the past but realize that I cannot live there, it is only a memory. With this thought in mind I can live in the present and think about a future. The counselor never judged me. He respected what I did, said, and felt. This gave me a feeling of contentment with my life up to now.

Does this anecdotal material, and similar testimonies of success, *prove* that our claim is true? No, we need more rigorous evaluation before we can seriously put forth a claim for absolutely greater efficacy for our method than for others.

But do our experiences—mine and those of colleagues who have been participating in this program for the past few years—*indicate* that it *might* be true?

I believe so.

I can't see any other meaning in the two main facts of the situation: first, that precious little is being done for mourners on a systematic consistent basis and under community auspices; and second, that the program of Pastoral Bereavement Counseling that we have initiated in New York has great potential for being introduced successfully into other communities.

For the first time in history, it is now realistically possible to launch a national movement that will actually alleviate the pain of grief and honestly heal the wounds of the bereaved.

In time, after our movement will have been established in a number of American communities, we will have a sufficient number of counselors and mourner-clients to set up a research project. We will then be in a position to test the validity of our design and the therapeutic efficacy of our recommended counseling techniques. It would even be possible to scientifically rate the value of particular techniques in particular situations.

In this volume we have tried to present the possibilities for healthy relief of grief. We see it as a high religious privilege to be partners with God in doing His work, *to heal the broken-hearted, and to bind up their wounds.*

BIBLIOGRAPHY

Becker, E. *The Denial of Death*. New York: Free Press, 1973.

Bloom, B.L. *Community Mental Health: A General Introduction*. Belmont, Calif.: Wadsworth Publishing, 1975.

Bowlby, J. *Loss: Sadness and Depression—Attachment and Loss*, Vol. III. New York: Basic Books, 1980.

Glick, I.O., Parkes, C.M., & Weiss, R. *The First Year of Bereavement*. New York: Basic Books, 1975.

Horowitz, M., Marmar, C., et al. *Personality Style and Brief Therapy*. New York: Basic Books, 1984.

Jackson, E.N., *Understanding Grief*. New York: Abingdon Press, 1957.

Jackson, E.N., *You and Your Grief*. New York: Hawthorn Books, 1961.

Kubler-Ross, E. *On Death and Dying*. New York: Macmillan, 1969.

Kutscher, A.H. (Ed.) *Death and Bereavement*. Springfield, Ill.: Thomas, 1969.

Lamm, M. *The Jewish Way in Death and Mourning*. London: Jonathan David, 1969.

Lasch, C. *Haven in a Heartless World: The Family Besieged*. New York: Basic Books, 1977.

Lewis, C.S. *A Grief Observed*. London: Faber & Faber, 1961.

Lifton, R.J. *The Broken Connection*. New York: Simon & Schuster, 1979.

Loewinsohn, J.L. *Survival Handbook for Widows*. Glenview, Ill.: Scott, Foresman & Co., 1984.

Osterweis, M., Solomon, F., & Green, M. *Bereavement: Reactions, Consequences, and Care*. Washington, D.C.: National Academy Press, 1984.

Parkes, C.M. *Bereavement*. London: Tavistock, 1972.

Parkes, C.M. *Bereavement: Studies of Grief in Adult Life*. New York: International Universities Press, 1972.

Parkes, C.M., & Weiss, R.S. *Recovery from Bereavement*. New York: Basic Books, 1983.

Pincus, L. *Death and the Family*. New York: Pantheon, 1974.

Raphael, B. *The Anatomy of Bereavement*. New York: Basic Books, 1983.

Schiff, H.S. *The Bereaved Parent*. New York: Penguin Books, 1977.

Schoenberg, B., Berger, I., et al. (Eds.) *Bereavement: Its Psychological Aspects*. New York: Columbia University Press. 1975.

Simos, B.G. *A Time to Grieve*. New York: Family Service Association, 1979.

Weiss, R. *Going It Alone: The Family Life and Social Situation of Single Parents*. New York: Basic Books, 1983.

Worden, J.W. *Grief Counseling and Grief Therapy: A Handbook for the Mental Health Practitioner*. New York: Springer, 1982.

APPENDIX

The Commission on Pastoral Bereavement Counseling was established in 1979 as an ecumenical association to be dedicated to the following purposes—

To awaken an interest among ministers, priests, and rabbis in the art of Pastoral Bereavement Counseling;

To recruit and train clergy and supervise their Pastoral Bereavement Counseling activities;

To educate and inform the general community about the usefulness and availability of this special counseling;

To establish local counseling centers where structured counseling to mourners can be offered as a community service.

The Founding Organizations at that time were: Calvary Hospital; Department of Health and Hospitals, Archdiocese of New York; Department of Pastoral Care, New York Council of Churches; Family Consultation Service, Archdiocese of New York; Hospital Apostolate, Archdiocese of New York; New York Board of Rabbis; The Hospital Chaplaincy, Inc.

The Commission on Pastoral Bereavement Counseling has conducted full-day Conferences on Bereavement and Bereavement Counseling at Adelphi University, at five major hospitals in the New York metropolitan area, in Staten Island, NY, Winston-Salem, NC, Miami and Ft. Lauderdale, FL.

The Commission has been represented at Bereavement Conferences in Jerusalem and Tel Aviv, Israel; at Washington DC; at Louisville, KY; at Denver, CO; at Corpus Christi, TX; at Paramus, NJ; at the annual Grief and Bereavement Conferences conducted by Yeshiva University in New York; and at the symposia and workshops offered by the Foundation of Thanatology at Columbia Presbyterian Hospital. The Director of the Commission has made many guest appearances on television and radio programs in furtherance of the Commission's aims.

The Commission has conducted 11 Training Courses for clergy and mental health practitioners. From 1984 to 1986, the Commission has certified 104 graduates of these 12-hour Training Courses as Counselor-Interns. With the cooperation of the social work departments of the participating hospitals, the Commission instituted a no-fee service to mourners of all denominations in the catchment areas of Beth Israel and Mt. Sinai Medical Centers in New York, and Booth Memorial Hospital in Flushing, Queens.

Since February 1987, the Commission has serviced those mourning an AIDS death at St. Clare's Hospital in New York City.

INDEX

137 (footnote), 149
the 10 recommended, 134
to be focused toward a goal,
65–66
Counselor attitudes, 149
acceptance, 69
love, 70, 71
needed for goal-directed
empathy, 53
needed for less
procrastination, 81
patience, 66–68, 149
tolerance, 68, 69, 149, 150
Counselor countertransference
dangers of, 85, 86
mitigating the dangers of, 86
Counselor's feelings
awareness of his own empathy,
72, 73
awareness of participating in
sacred enterprise, 77
indispensability of empathy,
38, 42, 122, 126, 148, 149,
153, 168
that may obstruct empathy,
135, 164–165
throughout the course of
therapy, 50
Counselor responses-illustrations
acceptance of mourner's
feelings, 113
assurance of normalcy, 112,
155
assurance of support, 151–153
commending mourner's
progress, 162–163
expressions of anger, 126,
156–157
identifying and labeling,
141–146
noting mourner's feelings, 113
reflection, 136–139

"staying with", 157
termination procedures, 169
"working through", 159–160
Counselor roles
as a companion in deep
feeling, 42, 130
as a shepherd, 39, 47
Counselor strategies
acceptance of mourner's fear
and helplessness, 123, 124
acceptance of the peripheral
emotions, 131
acknowledging mourner's deep
emotions, 116
assurance of normalcy, 111
for denial, 102–104
for numbness, 107
reflection, 112, 136–141
responding to mourner's
irrational anger, 125, 126
selecting specific techniques,
159 (footnote)
Course of therapy, 146
Current programs for mourners
inadequacy of, 42–44

Daydreaming, 20, 110, 111, 142
dynamics of, 110, 111
examples of, 111, 141–143
therapeutic response to, 112,
141–143
Denial
dynamics of, 100–102, 130–131
examples of, 102–104
therapeutic response to,
102–104, 131
Dynamics of
anger, 124, 125
assurance of support, 148–153
counselor countertransference,
85, 86
daydreaming, 110, 111